TH A NK I OU S

By Paul E González

Author: Paul E González Mangual

Contact the author:

say@thankious.com
www.paulgonzalez.net
Facebook /Thankious
Twitter   @Thankious

First edition: November 2015.
Design by Muuaaa Design Studio.
ISBN: 9781396494994-2

Printed in Colombia

I have to say
Thankiou to...

My Parents,
My Friends,
My Neighbors,
My Family,
My Ex-girlfriends,
My Teachers,
My College Professors,
My Mentors,
My Business Associates,
My Acquaintances,
My Colleagues,
My Fans,
My Facebook Friends,
My Twitter Followers,
My Actual Girlfriend,
My God,
Myself.

thank

+

you

=

thankiou

ABOUT THE BOOK

Thankious [thank + you] is a collection of positive bits and pieces that happen to all of us in a daily basis. The idea behind these notes is to express -through the written word- how thankful we are of the small and exceptional things that have a huge impact in life. Being thankful for the good, bad, weird and ordinary stuff that occur to us daily is more than an idea, it's a lifestyle. And this book is about living that lifestyle! Thankious is my way of immortalizing those moments of gratitude in a book that we can all enjoy, read while we are at the beach, when we are at a plane, just before bed or simply when we want a reason to smile.

Gratitude is expressed in a lot of ways, for example: friends with superpowers, secrets, midnight munchies, completed resolutions, for not knowing what tomorrow brings, free smiles and for the strangers that transform into family, among many others. There are a lot of reasons in life for which to be thankful and it has been scientifically proven that saying thankiou is directly related to the factors of happiness and the factors of solidarity. And before finishing reading this book, we have to say..

Thankiou!

"As we express our gratitude, we must never forget that the highest appreciation is not to utter words, but to live by them".

John F. Kennedy

THANKIOUS
1-12

Every now and then, we cruise life on autopilot hoping for the best. Along the way, certain situations makes us take turns and go in different directions. There are a lot of reasons as to why, for example: we don't love our jobs, we found a passion, it's a great opportunity or is necessary to start over from scratch. Starting something new is always scary but if we replace the fear of the unknown with curiosity, life simplifies. And before the new adventure becomes the journey of our dreams, we have to say...

Thankiou!

THANKIOU #2
THE FIRST DAY OF THE YEAR

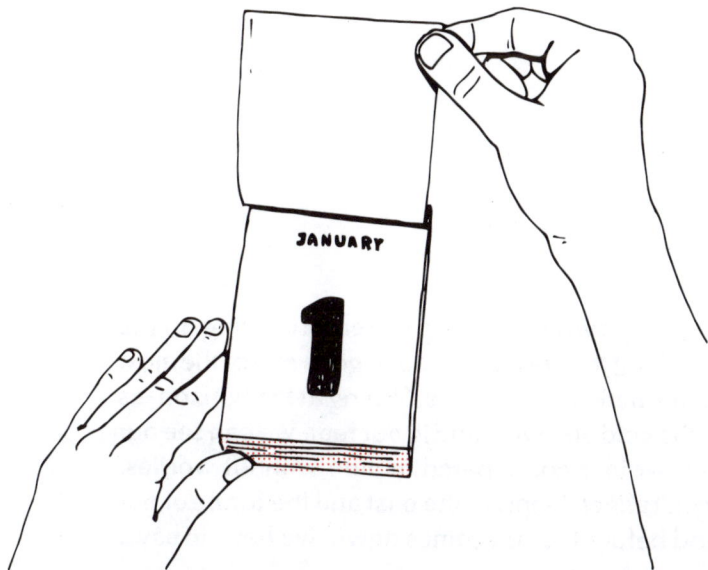

The first day of every new year is probably the longest one. It is almost a continuum of the previous year that keeps going after midnight. The day starts with an aura of celebration, happiness and never ending good feeling. We go to sleep for a bit and when we wake up, the family is all over the house ready to spend some more quality time and create new memories. And before the new year is over, we have to say...

Thankiou!

. . . .

THANKIOU #3
SITTING ON THE SAND

For some unknown psychological reason, sitting on the sand watching the waves come and go, is one of the most therapeutic activities there are. Staring at the horizon -as we feel the cold and wet sand in our feet- we can see our dreams flow in a coordinated motion without worries. Making us reflect deeply in the past and the future of our lives. And before the sun comes down, we have to say...

Thankiou!

. . . .

THANKIOU #4:
THE SILENCE INSIDE THE CAR

There's a mystical happening inside the car when you are driving alone and the radio is off. All of the sudden, silence rules, creating a temple of ease where the mind takes over. Thoughts become the designated driver and out of nowhere we find ourselves having a Q&A with ourselves. This is where life-changing decisions are made. And just when we think we might be going crazy, we have to say...

Thankiou!

THANKIOU #5
SONGS THAT EVERYONE KNOWS

Turn the volume up. The radio is on and without a notice, some random song starts. Very, very slowly and one by one, people around us start singing along. All of the sudden a mob concert commences. Chorus, a bit of dancing, a little air guitar, and everyone is on rock star mode. An unprecedented magnificent orchestra of family and friends creates a memory for the ages. And before the song ends, we have to say...

Thankiou!

. . . .

THANKIOU #6
THE MOMENT BETWEEN BEING AWAKE AND BEING ASLEEP

The sweet spot for creative thinking. A moment of total self-trust, imagination, without boundaries or uncontrollable circumstances. A moment when everything falls into place -mind, body, soul- and creates the perfect balance in the world. A moment where dreams are life-like and real life feels like a dream. A moment in which you wish you had someone to capture your thoughts in a blank canvas and preserve them forever. And for this inner peace that we feel just before we fall asleep, we have to say...

Thankiou!

. . . .

THANKIOU #7
NOT MAKING THE 8 BALL AND WINNING

For years, playing pool has been an amusing way for guys to bond and drink beer. Making eight balls with a wooden stick and six pockets seems like an easy task, but in reality it is a strategic game where the laws of physics play a huge role. There's always one guy in the group that knows all the tricks and always wins. We amateurs have to wait for the opportune moment when our opponent misses and puts the 8-Ball in the wrong pocket. It's not about us winning, but about him losing. And for his bad timing, we have to say...

Thankiou!

• • • • • • • •

THANKIOU #8
MALL HAPPENINGS

Big malls are more than shops. We can buy a pretzel there, window shop for shoes, be harassed by a phone company salesman and catch the latest movie. But it is the little things that make us come back each week: free air conditioning, kids dancing to an Xbox in the middle of the hall, car exhibitions, famous people walking by, water fountains, automatic staircases, interactive ad screens, music that comes out of every store, captivating lighting everywhere and a never-ending fashion show of pretty, old, professional, young, normal, tall, ugly or weird people. And before it closes, we have to look around and say...

Thankiou!

. . . .

THANKIOU #9
THE AROMA OF COFFEE

Around two-thirds of the world's population drinks coffee every day and the remaining third, at the very least, enjoys the glorious and invigorating perfume of freshly brewed coffee. Since its discovery in the ninth century, there is no doubt that coffee is a significant part of our lives. No kitchen, home or bakery is complete without its beguiling aroma in the morning. And while we sip and savor it, we have to say...

Thankiou!

. . . .

Helping others is a God-given gift. As humans, we have a monumental responsibility to make everything around us better. That means taking care of our family, friends and random people who we may bump into along the way that are in need of a helping hand. That is why one of the world's most inspirational, unselfish, heroic and heartening things is when a complete stranger offers to help us fix a flat tire without a reason, compensation or recognition. And for that unexpected helping hand, we have to say...

Thankiou

. . . .

THANKIOU #11
QUOTES ON WALLS

Have you ever found yourself taking a picture of a passage in some random wall? We have all done it. We have seen them in abandoned buildings, bathroom stalls, streets, advertisement agencies, trendy coffee shops and even in Marshall's and TJ Maxx. These are hints of brilliance that can be tweeted, smiled at and kept in mind for that personal meditation time. They give us a scope of people's mind and thoughts for us to guide our good and bad moments in life. And after we say our favorite quote, we have to say...

Thankiou!

There is a huge difference between saying "goodbye" and "see you later". Saying "goodbye" is the acknowledgment of parting, which is derived from the phrase "God be with you". On the other hand, saying "see you later" is a farewell with a second part coming soon. This to be continued will bring back all the fun, happy times and experiences shared together, at least for one more time. If we promise it, life will take care of the rest. And before we see each other again, we have to say...

Thankiou!

. . . .

THANKIOUS
13-27

THANKIOU #13
DAYS WHEN EVERYTHING GOES WRONG

Was today one of those days were you woke up on the wrong side of the bed? Was everything upside down, nothing went as planned and it felt like your world was crumbling down? Some days are just like that. The alarm didn't ring, you were late to a big presentation at work, had lunch at 4:00 p.m., the car broke down and when you got home there was no Internet. Before the day ends, you laid down in bed thinking about how crappy your day was, just to realize how fortunate you are to have a car, a cellular phone, food, a house, a job, family, friends, health and a lot of things you probably don't really need or use. And before we say 'shit happens', we have to say...

Thankiou!

. . . .

THANKIOU #14
HAVING FRIENDS OVER FOR NO REASON AT ALL

The best moments in life are unplanned. Sometimes we get that unexpected phone call from a childhood friend that wants to catch up, and suddenly, we get to ask them: 'Want to get together now?' And it happens. Beer comes and goes while talking about old friends, childhood memories, funny stories, girls, but most importantly, life. Nothing compares to the familiarity and ease that comes from someone that is more than a friend, he's family. And before that friend has to leave, we have to say...

Thankiou!

. . . .

Doesn't it feel bizarre when we reach for our watch and it reads 11:11? The real meaning of the 11:11 event is still a mystery. For astrologers, it is a reason to explain a mathematical mcoincidence of things that have or will occur in a lifetime. For normal people, it is an excuse to ask for a wish. The remarkable thing about this special figure is that it happens, not one, but two times a day giving us a unique opportunity to hope for something optimistic to be accomplished. Everything goes and anything comes during the 60 seconds it will last, so take your time and wish well. And before it's 11:12, we have to say...

Thankiou!

WRITE AND DRAW YOUR
THANKIOU _____

· · · · · · · ·

THANKIOU #16
MOMENTS

Life passes by in light speed mode, composed by a variety of vivacious moments. But there are a specific type of moments that are uniquely beautiful, and, therefore, more than special. Ever got that feeling that you are alone in a crowded place? That the world spins around you while standing still? In that precise moment, thoughts become the single voice, the only sound; and without notice -heart, soul and mind- start a deep conversation full of passion and truth. While we stare at infinity, the voices inside our head become existent, and for a moment, our true personality reveals itself. And before the moment ends, we have to say...

Thankiou!

. . . .

THANKIOU #17
THE LAST BITE

Eating is one of the life's most enjoyable pleasures. From the moment we start feeling hungry; to the moment we cook or order our food, to the grand finale of consumption. This bite represents the high point in a wonderful culinary adventure, as well as the defining moment of appetite satisfaction. It doesn't matter if the food was fantastic or terrible, or if we are hungry or full or have a specific desire for something, we will always go back to that last bite. And after that bite, we have to say…

Thankiou!

. . . .

Colorful characters with the sole purpose of making our day richer. These unusual individuals arrive at the most unpredictable moment when you find yourself needing them the most. We meet them at trendy restaurants, coffee shops, tea rooms, bars, dentist office's, airplanes, among a few others. Storytelling is their bread and butter, narrating stories about the past, citing history and explaining life's most controversial problems. It's unbelievable how much we can learn and be touched by the words of a complete stranger. And before the conversation ends, we have to say...

Thankiou!

. . . .

THANKIOU #19
CAR WASH TUNNELS

By the mid-1940s, the car wash era had just begun and started to become a nationwide trend. It's a very simple adventure: pay, enter the tunnel, get soaked, brushed, soaped, brushed again, soaked and blow dried. The most amazing thing about this automated activity is the time and the energy we save. Time and energy we can spend with the family, sleeping or enjoying a good cup of coffee. In a world without them, we would spend time and energy getting all the cleaning products, finding a spot, watering the car, hand brushing the soap, washing away the water and, finally, hand drying the entire car; which can take up to an hour or an hour thirty minutes versus a three minute trip. And before the car dries up, we have to say...

Thankiou!

Why are we so fascinated with space? The galaxy is filled with the unknown and the yet to be known. Luckily, every couple of years the Universe grants us with a half-bright, half-dark gift that's impossible to ignore. This astronomical event occurs when the Moon's shadow crosses the Earth's surface or when the Moon moves into the Earth's shadow. Either way, it captivates our most romantic side. And before we wake up in the middle of the night to see it, we have to say...

Thankiou!

A thankful mind is a magnet for positive vibes.

THE CALM AFTER BEING SCARED

Life is full of surprises and sometimes they are so frightening that makes us poop in our pants. Our existence is a continuum of opportunities of living and surviving in the jungle we call Earth. Crazy things can happen and it's the nervous system's job to keep it cool and guide us through any moment. After something terrifying happens -and everything is fine- we feel like we have been suddenly injected with peaceful molecules. And before we calmly rest, we have to say...

Thankiou!

. . . .

THANKIOU #22
FRIENDS WITH SUPERPOWERS

It's a bird...It's a plane...It's my friend! These very special people that have unique abilities and aptitudes that glow, even in the dark. They have the power to stop the tears, to make us smile, to inspire our every move, to help without rewards, and to get drunk by our side. They are giants amongst men. They speak and the world listens. They walk and the Earth trembles. Amazingly, they have no idea or are remotely aware of their superpowers; having been blinded be the misconceptions of the society and can only be seen through the eyes of someone else's heart. And before they figure it out, we have to say...

Thankiou!

Once in a while we attend a seminar that changes our lives. Once in a while we get moved by the words of a persuasive speaker. Once in a while we get hit by a reality bus that dares us to act. But by the end of it, we are fueling our minds and getting our creative juices flowing. Ideas come and go, and we know it's time to be remarkable. It's time to put plans in motion and achieve what we all deserve. Getting psyched is just the first stepping stone in creating a better world for everyone. And somewhere in between, we have to say...

Thankiou!

THANKIOU #24
DAD'S COOKING

Grandma's and mom's cooking are delicious. They are definitely award-winning comfort food. We can't live without it, we constantly miss it and travel miles just to eat it. On the other hand, dads have a couple of marquee dishes that are mouth-watering as well. When it comes to BBQ, grilled stuff, red meat, cocktails and paellas, it's definitely a man's world. They may not be like the fancy chefs on TV or generational recipe holders, but they are specialized cooks that understand the complexity of their plates. Their secret ingredient: love. And we must admit that it's a different kind of love. And before dinner is ready, we have to say...

Thankiou!

GOING WITH THE FLOW

Sometimes we think WAY too much. Thinking is a human trait and is completely necessary, but it doesn't take us anywhere unless we do something with it. We can talk about ideas, feeling or dreams but as long as we don't take a chance, we won't benefit from the outcome. The fear of failure plays a protagonist role in the over thinking process, but fear's kryptonite is to risk it all and hope for the best. Every so often, it's better to go with the flow of life and enjoy the ride. And before flowing away, we have to say...

Thankiou!

. . . .

THANKIOU #26
NOT HAVING ENOUGH TIME

The digital revolution is upon us, people need information faster, technology changes every instant and time flies by. There is no time to stop. Calendars have been extended from 365 to 730 days, days from 24 to 48 hours and hours from 60 to 120 minutes. Feels like life is skipping a beat and missing the big picture. But, why don't we have enough time? It's simple: we have a full-time job, family to take care of, friends to socialize, a house to clean, a side business, a childhood hobby, a leadership position on a civic organization, activities to attend to and someone to spoil and love. Not having enough time is... beautiful. And before we gain more time, we have to say...

Thankiou!

. . . .

The precise moment in which destiny is fulfilled. The stars don't always align as we wish, and most of the time it's because of bad timing. The person we love just got married, the business we want to start is way ahead of its time, our dream job has eliminated the position we were interested in because of economic problems, the restaurant we were salivating about closed 10 minutes earlier. We can receive all this signs as negative energy but it is the Universe's way of saying: your time is not right now; but with a little faith and patience, it will be worth the wait. And before that particular moment arrives, we have to say...

Thankiou!

THANKIOUS
28-37

There is no better reason than to be thankful for no reason at all. This day resides in an unparalleled gap between the first day of the week and the one not far away from the magical weekend. Although its name comes from the Old English word "Tiwesdæg", which literally means "Tiw's Day or second day, it's actually the third day of our modern week. In mythology, the term means the god of single combat and victory. So, no matter the circumstances the day brings, let's keep battling our way through the week enjoying each day, one at a time. And before Wednesday arrives, we have to say...

Thankiou!

. . . .

THANKIOU #29
BEING SINGLE

Yes, finding love is one of life's main purposes. Being single, it's not about boycotting love, hanging out like a maniac or not responding to anyone. Being single, it's about finding ourselves, understanding what we want to accomplish, prioritizing our goals and dreams, but most importantly, learning to live by ourselves. Not depending on others, gives us the liberty to explore life's complications, meet thousands of people and travel to the depth of our mind and heart. Being single, is magical. And before we find our soulmate, we have to say...

Thankiou!

DREAMING OF WINNING THE LOTTERY

It's a one in a trillion chance, but it could happen. What would you do with it? How would you spend it? Some of us will buy expensive luxurious cars, penthouses, go on a shopping spree, and start our retirement plans. Others will choose the road less traveled and settle all of the family debts, create college trust funds for young family members, help out a few friends, make generous donations to some non-profit organizations, create a savings account or invest in a couple of ventures. It doesn't matter what we do with the money, the important thing is to remember where we came from, the people that formed us and never changing. And before the winning numbers are announced, we have to say...

Thankiou!

. . . .

Showing **gratitude** is one of the simplest yet most powerful things humans can do for each other.

Randy Paulsh

THANKIOU #31
SHARING DREAMS

Once upon a time, a great man shared his dream and changed history as we know it. Since then, every time someone shares a dream life makes a little more sense. When we speak about them, people stop to hear, to analyze and to contribute. They introspect of their own dreams and have an urge to share them as well. Dreams are the unspoken motor on the world, it is what drive us; so let's never stop dreaming. And before it becomes a reality, we have to say...

Thankiou!

. . . .

THANKIOU #32
FOR WHAT WE DON'T SAY

Imagine yourself at 80 years old, sitting in a rocking chair while looking back at life's good and bad moments. Would you wish to have said things you didn't? Done things you didn't have the chance to do? Any regrets? Life is one big decision after another, with no instruction book or roadmap. We just need to go out there, without holding back and pour our heart in every move. What's the worst that could happen? We will just keep living. And before we say what needs to be said, we have to say...

Thankiou!

· · · · · · · ·

THANKIOU #33
SPORTS THAT UNITE NATIONS

A lot of negative things -war, politics, dead, riots- can unite people in the same cause, but it's refreshing when beauty pageants, artists and sports can do it as well. Every country has at least one national sport with many world-known athletes. Every four years, some kind of global tournament turns its people into TV zombies watching their national team/athlete, game after game. Even smaller events, like boxing matches, can have an electrifying effect on their citizens, so immense, that their sports heroes are received with a magnificent celebration parade, even if the outcome wasn't the expected one. Win or lose, these events make us proud of our hometowns and, eventually, our love for them grows. And for all of our countries heroes, we have to say...

Thankiou!

THANKIOU #34
BEING SICK

Am I out of mind? Not really. When you think about it, being sick is a routine disrupter. Without a notice, our jam packed schedule is suddenly empty, leaving enough time to rest, sleep and eat. We may not feel like running a race or attending a party, but we have sufficient energy to do what we daydream about doing when we are at work: watching TV, being in pajamas all day, eating cereal out of the box, getting a hot water bath and doing just nothing at all. Having a cold can suck, but there is nothing like having a mini-vacation in the middle of high season. And before we get better, we have to say...

Thankiou!

. . . .

BIG PICTURE: restaurant, bar, bartender, hot girl or boy at the end of the bar, loud music, bread, five plasma TV's with sports, people hanging out, and a weird guy to the right. That's the ideal panorama for a night between friends and hard liquor, but not always. Sometimes we can just sit, relax and enjoy a good read. The fascinating thing about reading at a crowded place is that your brain creates an invisible bubble that blocks distractions, allowing you to get lost in the words. At that moment, time stops completely and transports us to our own little world. And before the chapter ends, we have to say...

Thankiou!

THANKIOU #36
SHARING LIFE

There's an old motto that says we came to this world alone and we are going out the same way we came. But we have to be honest with ourselves, there's no meaning in living alone. The best moments in life are produced when we are surrounded by people we love. It's liberating to call up a friend and talk to him for about 10, 20, 30 minutes about the person we like. It's invigorating to plan a family trip with the folks. It's remarkable to share successes with business partners. It's extraordinary to share a meal with that special someone. And before the next life, we have to say...

Thankiou!

DISCOUNTED DISCOUNTS

Shopping is a necessary evil that we do as a form of entertainment, pleasure or necessity. The sensation of finding or buying something new gives us the butterflies. Sadly, we cannot buy everything we see or want, but discounts make it possible. Even better, if the discounted good has an additional discount on it, it's a perfect matchup. In the shopping world, discounts are the magic trick that turn butterflies into the 'I cannot live without it' attitude. And before we max out our credit card, we have to say...

Thankiou!

· · · · · · · · ·

THANKIOUS
38-51

They say that the best things in life are free. It's very endearing when a stranger in the street looks us in the eyes and gives us a big smile. When we reciprocate, everyone's eyes light up; and, in a matter of seconds, our cheeks fill up and fuel the day with freshly baked emotions. We are probably never seeing that person again, but our destinies were crossed and completely fulfilled. Remember that smiling is a simple act of kindness, with no cost and with vast dividends; so let's give and spread the good vibes. And before we get to see that person again, we have to say...

Thankiou!

THANKIOU #39
GLOBAL MOVEMENTS

The world is flat again. We live in an era were nothing is out of reach, information is a click away, China and Spain are neighbors and nothing is impossible. In times like these, Martin Luther King would have persuaded the Earth with his words, Gandhi would have been heard in every corner of the Planet and Madre Theresa's work would have echoed the Universe. Today, certain causes can unite the world in an unimaginable way. It's unbelievable how millions and millions of strangers can share the love for a particular reason. Small dues can contribute into a larger picture and its feels good to be a part of it. And before the next movement, we have to say...

Thankiou!

. . . .

They tell the story of simpler times. There are so many types of bulbs nowadays - incandescent, fluorescent, halogen, LED, that we have completely forgotten were everything started. When was the last time you lighted up a candle? Probably, a long time ago. Every now and then, we should turn the lights out and turn on a couple of candles, and just stare at them. Their relaxing flame and smell will make us feel like the old days when the night looked sinister and romantic at the same time. And before the wax melts, we have to say...

Thankiou!

. . . .

THANKIOU #41
NAP TIME

Remember in kindergarten when nap time was part of the school day? Well, the Spaniards really remember it. Each day, as a cultural tradition, they take a siesta early afternoon were everyone shuts down businesses, offices and welcome the sleeping king. Do you imagine a power nap in your workplace? That would be splendid. Even studies show that a brief period of sleep during work hours can actually boost productivity, lower stress and make employees happier. With a mandated everyday nap time, work will never be the same. And before applying for a Spanish citizenship, we have to say...

Thankiou!

. . . .

THANKIOU #42
THINKING ABOUT SOMEONE

It's a great feeling to know that there are people who think of us in the most special way. But when we are the ones who are thinking of that special someone, it is a bigger deal. We tend to fantasize about spending time together, wishing you can both be hanging out watching movies or simply sipping coffee at a restaurant. Soon, everything will materialize and become our reality, we'll be together and making up for lost time. And before we pick them up at the airport, we have to say...

Thankiou!

THANKIOU #43
PLANNING VACATIONS

It's that time of the year again. We start to get excited and start planning, planning, and planning. First, we need to ask for days off at work, then we pick a place, create a budget and start buying tickets for everything. We ask everyone where to go and what was their experience. Almost a month before, we find ourselves searching for things to do, shows to see, attractions we can't miss, restaurants to eat and historical sites to visit. A couple of days before we go, we start drooling and daydreaming about what we are going to be doing soon; and it's the best feeling in the world. And before vacations start, we have to say...

Thankiou!

From time to time, life likes to play the tick tock game in certain situations to test our human spirit. It only takes one player and an imagination full of hope and desire towards something or someone. We sit and wait for a magical thing to happen. It could be a job opportunity, a test score, a date, love, summer vacations or Christmas for the heart to burst with emotion. Waiting develops the abilities of the ancient gods: patience, wisdom, truth and glory. Even if we wait for days or even years, the outcome -without considering the result- is the finest reward. And before the time comes, we have to say...

Thankiou!

. . . .

Repeat:

I am grateful for today.

There are a couple of special days each year where families come together. The main purpose: to eat. Bonding, catching up, seeing nephews, grandparents and out of town relatives is great any day of the year, but having a table full of food and sharing with them is a religious experience. While eating, old stories are told, jokes come and go, bottles of wine are opened and bellies are filled until exploding. Life is better enjoyed surrounded by people we love. And before the next get together, we have to say...

Thankiou!

THANKIOU #46
THE WOW FACTOR

Mesmerized. Electrified. Astonished. There are unique moments in life when we are blown away by them. It could be by something wicked, a miracle, a gorgeous lady or an out of this world happening. In that precise moment, the only thing the mind can actually say is 'wow'. That electrifying feeling of surprise is followed by an unpredictable fantasy that becomes real. There is no doubt we have been swept of our feet without a notice. And before we go back into neutral, we have to say...

Thankiou!

. . . .

THANKIOU #47
VIRTUAL SOCIALIZATION

It could be the hottest day ever, we could be hit by the biggest storm or it could be pouring out rain for three days straight and it wouldn't be an impediment to hang out with friends and family. Socializing virtually gives us the opportunity to experience real life human interaction in the comfort of our homes. We could tell jokes, express feelings, share songs and videos, distribute news and events, play games in teams and even chat face to face. Technology and social media has narrowed the gap of social life by enhancing it over the Internet. The power to be interconnected with friends, family and folks all over the world is beyond belief. And before the next big thing, we have to say...

Thankiou!

THANKIOU #48
LEFTOVERS

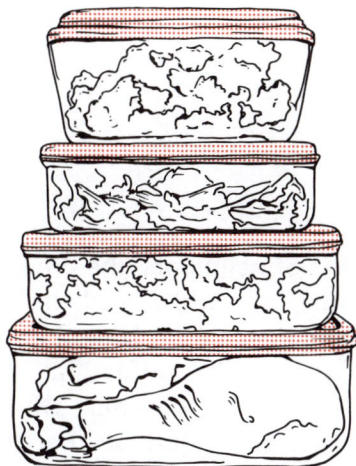

After a big feast in a restaurant or home, there are sometimes just enough scraps for the next day. In the American culture, we plan food consumption based on potential attendee's and overestimate just in case more people show up. Some of us don't mind eating the same food over and over again. Over the course of 24 to 48 hours, these provisions are being aged to perfection. Leftovers are the preserved beauty of a past food memory. If it tasted good the first day, it's a known fact that the next would be even better. And before the leftovers perish, we have to say...

Thankiou!

. . . .

There are two kinds of neighbors: the ones we salute politely, every once in a while, and the ones who become our acquaintances. It's uncomfortable taking the elevator with unfamiliar neighbors that only talk about the weather. Occasionally, there is an unpredictable situation that transforms this awkward exchanges into meaningful conversations. They may not be family or longtime friends, but it's always good to know that someone near knows our name. And when the turnaround from alien to friend happens, we have to say...

Thankiou!

THANKIOU #50
FEELING PRETTY DAY

Once every blue moon, we wake up on the good side of the bed and the ambiance has an invigorating glow. We look at the mirror and all we can see is the image of perfection, the synonym of stunning, the reincarnation of Aphrodite and Narcissus. Walking on the street we feel like we are hovering all over the place, turning heads in every corner, everyone is smiling at us and the world could be persuaded with the beauty we expel. But it's all an illusion, we feel beautiful because we are under the influence of the happiness factor. And before reality checks in, we have to say...

Thankiou!

. . . .

Diaries know our stories. Night after night, they embrace our problems and understand our decisions. More than a confident, they are our fortress of secrets and confessions, the guardians of our soul, a personal psychologist that hears everything and the soft comforting ear that has all the answers. They have the power to absorb our words and transform them into dreams. Writing on a diary is an alternate, yet functional, and acceptable way of talking to God. And before we fall asleep, we have to say...

Thankiou!

THANKIOUS
52-68

Stories could be told with a single stare. Sadness, happiness and love are mixed together in everyone's eyes. If we are lucky enough, and we get to look intently at someone's eyes, we can experience seeing two blistering crystals that glow and transcend words. It's not every day that the world can shine as bright as love can. From blink to blink, there are times when the heart wants to pop out and scream something beautiful. And before those eyes close, we have to say...

Thankiou!

THANKIOU #53
EATING ALONE

Why not? There are a lot of life experiences that can be enjoyed unaccompanied. Jogging, shopping, watching a movie, playing video games, reading, eating and singing are some of them. Of all of those, eating alone is a very distinctive one because most of us feel very uncomfortable doing it. Rarely we see someone at a restaurant by their own, but it shows independence, confidence and courage. It can also be a little playful, we tend to create a two way conversation within ourselves thinking about things to do, things to remember and places to go. And before the next culinary adventure, we have to say...

Thankiou!

Life is all about establishing relationships. Cultivating a healthy amount of friends and acquaintances is the core of any successful job hunt, Saturday night or business venture. It has its perks, for example, have you ever gone to a place and just about everyone knows you? Do you get the feeling that you are the Mayor? Being recognized is something to be treasured because with all certainty we are doing something right or meaningful. Being almost famous means more than having a prestigious status in society or having a million dollar contract. It is a way to develop relationships with people and get to call them extended family. And before our Hollywood star is presented, we have to say...

Thankiou!

THANKIOU #55
FLIRTING VIA TEXT MESSAGES

Love is in the air. Texting has become the digital revolution tool for 21 century Romeo's and Juliet's. The wait, the intrigue and the suspense that's built from text to text, give the spark needed to get to know another person without too much words. Texts are short and sweet, so they get to the point fast. We went from walking to the house to telegrams to mail-in letters to telephone calls to emails to text messages; it's the way of a fast-paced, information frenzy community. No matter how impersonal they might sometimes be, they still feel like 160 characters poems. And before the next one arrives, we have to say...

Thankiou!

. . . .

The Holstee Manifesto reads: life is about the people you meet and the things you create with them, so go out and start creating. Now, stop and think about those moments. What have we created? What memory still lives deep in our hearts? How happy were we while living them? There's nothing better than recollecting memories in silence and smiling about them. That's one of life's most precious rewards. So, what's next? And before more extraordinary moments pile up, we have to say...

Thankiou!

THANKIOU #57
WHEN THE BRAIN CAN'T STOP THINKING

Symptoms: can't think straight, deep feeling of disbelief, sleep deprived, high levels of ADD, among others. Although all that symptoms can come and go, it's great to feel alive. When the brain doesn't stop, we see life in a very particular and detailed manner. We get analytical, poetic, thoughtful, imaginative; and, it's all part of a very sophisticated plan -between the mind, soul and body- to create something pure and extraordinary. The only way to stop it, is to face the fear, thing or person that's keeping us awake and simply live by it. And before the sleeping pills take effect, we have to say...

Thankiou!

THANKIOU #58
UNCOORDINATED DANCING

Dancing is the body's way to express happiness. There are three main reasons as to why do it: peer pressure, we love it or just because it's fun. The best reason for it is to simply have fun and enjoy it. Moving our feet without thinking or following a choreography is liberating. It's not about knowing the right move and speed, it's about having the right attitude to feel free. And before the next song, we have to say...

Thankiou!

HOW MANY
TIMES
CAN WE SAY
THANKIOU
IN
1 DAY?

Meet-up places are points of encounter. These places are for unofficial social clubs that friends and fools use to get together, chat, drink, and have a good time. These venues can vary according to the person's social class, age, and lifestyle. Groups can meet during breakfast, coffee breaks, lunch or after work almost every day of the week. It doesn't matter when or where, there's is always a familiar face to share life with. It is in this unique spot where big cities don't feel intimidating and where they have that small town sentiment in which everyone knows our name. And before we meet up again, we have to say...

Thankiou!

THANKIOU #60:
A DEEP BREATH

"Life is not measured by the number of breaths we take but by the amount of moments that take our breath away", they say. Deep breaths are one of the few ways the soul uses to smile about a particular blissful moment. They are evidence that we are living life passionately. Unfortunately, they only last a few seconds, but the reasons for its happening can last a lifetime. When love is the reason of a deep breath occurrence, be especially sure that the heart is skipping a beat. Stay on the lookout for these unique moments, for they could be extraordinary. And before we breathe out, we have to say...

Thankiou!

THANKIOU #61
MOVIES THAT INSPIRE

Motion pictures have all the elements -music, drama, action, pictures, characters, colors- to arouse our intellect and dreams. Some movies can turn out to be more than a two-hour entertainment, they can become a reason to start new adventures. We know when a certain film is out of the ordinary, when we start quoting specific sayings and moments that marked us. It doesn't matter how real or fictional a movie can be, if it fits in the imagination, it fits on reality. And before the movie ends, we have to say...

Thankiou!

. . . .

WRITE AND DRAW YOUR
THANKIOU _____

_____

_____

_____

_____

_____

. . . .

Since the day we are born we have been taught with typical customs and traditions of our hometowns. Music routines, food recipes, holiday festivities and religious rituals are some of the rituals employed by almost everyone born in the nation. Every time we celebrate one of these traditions, we feel part of history. Sometimes we have no clue who created it, why they were formed or how and when they began, but the pleasure generated from embracing traditions gives us a powerful reason to be connected with our people and country. And before some traditions are forgotten, we have to say...

Thankiou!

. . . .

THANKIOU #63
STUPID IDEAS

Forest Gump famous saying "stupid is as stupid does", indicates that a person is judged stupid by the stupid acts they commit; but we are as stupid as we let our imagination fly away. Is in the stupid things that life starts making sense. Christopher Columbus was stupid enough to sail into the end of the earth, just to find a whole new world. In business and in life, we need to start trying new things, fail continuously, learn from our mistakes, and in the process, become stronger human beings. And before more stupid ideas come to mind, we have to say..

Thankiou!

. . . .

THANKIOU #64
FOOD TRUCKS

We are living a culinary revolution on wheels. Food trucks are mobile kitchens that serve gourmet sensations in the most peculiar places. We can find any type of food there: Chinese food, Mexican food, ice cream, yogurt, hot dogs, burgers, pizza, amongst many others. Chic or rustic, they fill the need for a delicious delicacy in small portions and cheap prices. Every time we find out about a new food truck, instead of researching how good it is, we just go out to try it. The experience lies in finding it, making the line, and eating the food at the corner of the street. And before we open our own food truck, we have to say...

Thankiou!

. . . .

THANKIOU #65
FINISHING TO-DO LISTS

So much to do, so little time. When busy, the superlative thing to do is to write down everything, make a list and prioritize. To-do lists can be stressful because they show the things we still need to finish while we are multitasking with other ones. In between tasks, due dates and deadlines have to be met in order to stay on top of our personal life, job or business. There's no argument that when we cross off every item in the list and fully complete it, we experience an immense sensation of accomplishment, relief and tranquility. And before new tasks arrive, we have to say...

Thankiou!

. . . .

THANKIOU #66
AIRPLANE WINDOWS

Nothing says live entertainment like watching life through a window. When we are 38,000 feet above the sea level, everything looks quite different. From the sky we can see the clouds, patches of land in the sea, a black spot that hints to be space, and when arriving at our destinations, parts of the country that are not showcased in tourism magazines. The small acrylic glass, from where we get a glance of everything, is the only thing separating us from infinity. And before we land, we have to say...

Thankiou!

THANKIOU #67
SAYING I MISS YOU

Love can be a very complicated and tricky business. But saying some specific phrases can ease its overall understanding and complexity. Saying I miss you, is the heart's way of saying he needs to recharge itself with some human contact. This phrase is one of the shortest and most powerful poems we can dedicate to loved ones. Beware, when we say it, the receiving party will automatically smile and blush. And before we see them, we have to say...

Thankiou!

. . . .

There are almost 7 billion people distributed in 196 countries and 7 continents. The chances we end up exchanging experiences with a few of them are zero to none. That's why, we need to treasure every chance we get in meeting new people because odds are we are probably never seeing them again. In our lifetime, we are bound to meet an average of about 10,000 people. The most important thing is to seize every moment, fulfill each other's purpose and the few that stay in our lives will become extended family. And before we become friends, we have to say...

Thankiou!

. . . .

THANKIOUS
69-82

TV series tend to capture our attention, time and hearts. Most series are really addictive because the script is very well written, we can relate it to our story and we enjoy watching the ironic side of life. These shows can be unique and have somewhat controversial themes, for example, sarcastic comedies, political controversy, terrorism, historical moments or racial dramas. Good or bad, their time on air greatly depends on how deep the connection is between the characters and us. And before the new season premier, we have to say...

Thankiou!

· · · · · · · ·

THANKIOU #70
THE PERFECT GIFT

We can spend hours or even days searching for an ideal present for a special person. First, we brainstorm their likes and dislikes, hobbies, what they already have and what they use; narrowing down the ideas. Then, cleverly ask a few questions to test the waters and have an inside perspective of the best things from the list to choose from. Finally, we go the mall and search all over the place for the things that will make them 'WOW'. Always in the most unpredictable place, on an isolated corner, we found it standing alone and glowing like it belongs to us. Bingo! And before the next special occasion, we have to say...

Thankiou!

. . . .

THANKIOU #71
APPLAUDING UPON ARRIVAL

The act of clapping is as old and as widespread as humanity. Striking the palms of the hands together, quickly and repeatedly, is a way to express appreciation for some kind of performance. These can be music concerts, speeches, plays or plane arrivals at airports. Curiously, Puerto-Rican and Italian citizens have a popularized culture to applaud captains and their crews for the successful landing of an aircraft. Although the risk of a plane crashes is very low, Latin cultures tend to be a little more superstitious than the rest of the World. That why in this case, clapping is more than an act of gratitude, is the celebration of life. And before the next takeoff, we have to say...

Thankiou!

THANKIOU #72
HOME SWEET HOME

There is no place like home. Our bed, moms homemade comfort food, the smell, old toys, family pictures hanging on the wall, the cat running around and the feeling of love in the air, are just a couple of perks about being at home. This house –the one we probably grew up in- is our nest, our secure zone, our bunker of tranquility and the place where we can turn our engines off. This is the one place were memories lay in every corner, literally and symbolically. And before diner is ready, we have to say...

Thankiou!

The world is a mysterious place, full of unresolved matters, undefined things and unexplored places. There is a specific set of idiosyncratic matters that can help comprehend our surroundings, they are indigenous rituals, physics, finding love, having a new born, creating a disruptive technology that changes the course of life, talking to ourselves and finding answers, death and reading books. Although the beauty of life -most of the time- relies on its mystery, we should create a balance between what we understand and what we should never know. And before life reveals itself in front of our eyes, we have to say...

Thankiou!

THANKIOU #74
BEVERAGES WITH HISTORY

Can you imagine when the monks brewed and tasted the first beer? Or when a farmer in Ethiopia roasted the first coffee bean? Humanity's history can be told by the beverages we elaborate, drink and use. The World's biggest decisions were -and still are- centered on a table with coffee, tea or a glass of wine. Every day we sit among friends or family with some type of beverage in hand and we are discussing important life-changing topics; we are echoing those historic moments like our ancestors. Can you imagine life without them? And before the next cup or glass, we have to say...

Thankiou!

THANKIOU #75
SHOUTING AT THE OCEAN

AAAAaaaahhhh!!! What a crazy thing to do, but it makes a lot of sense. There are a lot of reasons to shout at the ocean: it is liberating, therapeutic, sometimes it is good to be heard and, the truth is, the ocean is a great secret keeper. People might look at us in a weird way, but they know deep in their hearts that it is a courageous and often necessary thing to do. Every once in a while, everyone should scream their lungs out at the ocean and see what life brings. And before the next shouting match, we have to say...

Thankiou!

ONE
THANKIOU
can change
the world.

We can plan and try to control everything around us, but sometimes the best things in life are unplanned. Improvising a particular situation is never going to be disappointing because we are getting more that we actually expected. If we add the family into the equation, the result multiplies and becomes infinite. Catching up wlth the people we love the most in this world is as beautiful as life can get. Is in moments like this that we experience immortality. And before the next unplanned gathering, we have to say...

Thankiou!

THANKIOU #77
THE CLOUDS

Remember when we were kids and clouds were far, far away? They were the only thing between Earth and outer space. We all dreamed with someday touching them and sleeping in their puffy comfort. Now we know they are more than floating marshmallows, they are important pillars of life's water cycle and the people's protector from the sun god Apollo. And before being up in the air, we have to say...

Thankiou!

. . . .

The Babel tower myth is coming alive once again. People from different backgrounds, cultures, religions and races are joining forces in a diversity of environments. You know the world has become one big unit when a Chinese woman is serving food at an Italian joint. Humanity is the biggest and largest organization in the Universe and we should all be part of its glory. The days of racial discrimination or slowly fading away. And before we marry a Colombian goddess, we have to say...

Thankiou!

. . . .

THANKIOU #79
THE SNOOZE BUTTON

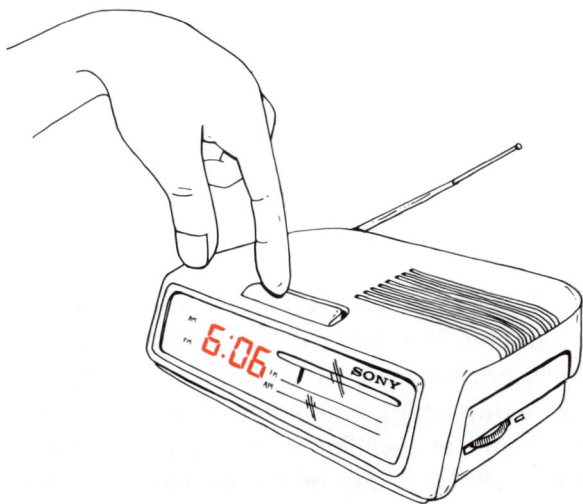

Ten minutes in heaven. For all of us who are not morning persons, we should get together and build a monument for the one who invented the snooze button. This little extra time of sleep will define how the day goes by and will be the difference between a smile and a frown. Snoozing is a great way to prolong dreams. It's during this purgatory that time and space dance together before celebrating a new God-given day. And before we wake up, we have to say...

Thankiou!

. . . .

When there is a will, there is a way. Haiti is a brother to all American countries. They live in extreme circumstances but hopefully not for long. An avalanche of helping hands are establishing themselves in the root of their land and are willing to go deep into their hearts. There will be a day when we can say, just as with Rome, that Haiti wasn't rebuilt in a day. And before more help comes their way, we have to say...

Thankiou!

THANKIOU #81
FOR HAVING NO WORDS

Once every blue moon, life surprises us in unimaginable ways. This is the moment when a certain something comes from nowhere and wakes up our most poetic personality. Although everything may scream loudly inside, no words come out of our mouths. The only communication channels are the eyes, smiles, and lips. And before words come back from vacation time, we have to say...

Thankiou!

. . . .

Math class teaches us numbers, equations and theorems that are infinite, but life also teaches us moments, ideas and experiences that are infinite. Infinite is derived from the Latin infinitas, which can be translated as "unboundedness", meaning that there are no boundaries that can hold back illusions, goals or dreams to ever come true. For centuries, mankind has tried to reach it, but love is the only way to get close to it. As a modus vivendi, let's go out every day to infinity and beyond! And before infinity isn't so far out, we have to say...

Thankiou!

THANKIOUS
83-99

THANKIOU #83
WHERE EVERYTHING STARTED

Every living thing, nation, place, sport, tradition and organization has a birth place, some have been around for thousands of years while others are bound to come alive in a future time. This point of origin is more than a place, it is a reason for remembering and a motive for celebrating in a continuous basis. Do we know where our best friend friendship started? Or where the spark of a lover ignited? More than a tangible answer, it was -and still is- the start of something beautiful. And before everything ends, we have to say...

Thankiou!

THANKIOU #84
FEELING LIKE IN A MOVIE

If it fits in the imagination, it shall fit in reality. Every movie ever made is based in something: true events, imagination, dreams or ordinary occurrences. Rarely in life, we get the feeling we are living inside a romantic comedy, action, drama or sitcom, but when it happens it's an out of this world feeling. Hallucination plays a huge role. Sometimes we envision walking over a red carpet, with camera flashes all over the place and magazine covers mentioning us; but the reality isn't a far fetch dream, all we need to do is to bring our character to life. And before the movie premiers, we have to say…

Thankiou!

. . . .

THANKIOU #85
PHONES WITH INTERNET

Literally, the world in the palm of our hands. The Internet has revolutionized the way we communicate, search for information and socialize with friends. Our world is so interconnected that coffee shop debates and bar talks have completely changed from heated discussions to Google searching. Every topic can be substantially argued with verified information in an instant, leaving mystery and doubt as a thing of the past. At the same time, this fast and simple access to information can help us connect more with someone we just met. And before we lose our signal, we have to say...

Thankiou!

. . . .

THANKIOU #86
HELIUM

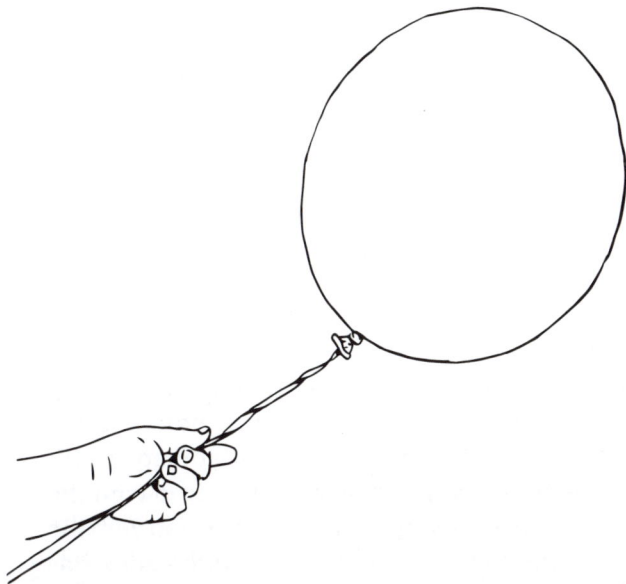

Remember when we were kids and a balloon was all we needed to play and have fun? This colorful round creation is filled with an odorless, tasteless, non-toxic, monoatomic gas that makes them float like magic. It is named after the Greek Sun god Helios, which perfectly explains why balloons want to reach the sky and head out to space. Love has the same effect as helium, it fills our hearts with a magical chemical that make us fly away. And before the balloon pops, we have to say...

Thankiou!

. . . .

When the muse strikes, the words flow with ease. Nothing can stop us from writing, writing and writing whatever thought comes to mind. But there is a big secret behind every muse: a special someone. It's unbelievable how every question is answered with the perfect response and every sentence is finished with the right words. Throughout history, being in the zone has inspired the greatest novels, poems, songs, artworks and kisses. And before we lose the moment, we have to say...

Thankiou!

THANKIOU #88
THE DAY WE WERE BORN

After nine months, we finally saw the light. The day we were born marks a special moment because it's the start of a new legend. Nobody has a clue what destiny has in place for this newborn, but as God's children, we are intended for greatness. There is a very low chance we remember this particular event, but we will never forget the tears of joy of the one person who made it possible: our mother. She put everything on the line to welcome us to the real world. And for the rest of our lives, we have to say...

Thankiou!

Brazilian author, Paulo Coelho, wrote: "I think God talks to us through signs, which are a special language we can only learn through belief and language". In order to see the signs, we have to pay close attention to our surroundings at every moment. They can appear in a book, through a bird's melody, a random happening, while meeting someone or find something, among other things. This is God's code to communicate, at the right moment, with us mortals. If we are aware of our intuition and daily coincidences, we can live fuller and richer lives. And before the next sign, we have to say...

Thankiou!

. . . .

There is no better reason to be **thankful** than for no reason at all.

THANKIOU #90
MULTITASKING

Human beings have complicated life so much that doing just one thing at a time is not fulfilling. Life's pace has gone to such a high level that we need to multitask to feel productive. Sometimes we find ourselves cooking, watching TV, doing laundry, surfing the web and talking on the phone, all at the same time. Is this some kind of superpower? Kind of, this quality has been inherited from our moms and grandmas; they were the ones who started this fad when they had the responsibility to maintain the household and work at the same time. The best thing: they did it without complaining and for love. And before taking a break, we have to say...

Thankiou!

THANKIOU #91
RUSH HOUR

It's time to get things done. Almost every day has 60 minutes in which craziness is unveiled to the world and stress takes control of everything. In just one hour, we produce more than what we do in an eight-our shift. In a blink of an eye, the email inbox is emptied, the to-do lists are marked done, tasks are distributed, and doubts are answered. Once everything is completed, we get a feeling of accomplishment and reward for all the hard work. And before we procrastinate a little bit, we have to say...

Thankiou!

Songs may understand how we feel at a certain point, but poetry expresses how our soul feels. Reading or writing it, either way, is liberating. When someone writes a poem it's all about pouring out the deepest emotions and feelings, with the most heated passion, in a black and white canvas. The connection level becomes so high that the pen and the paper becomes our confidants and best friends. Poetry is the encrypted language to translate words into true love. And before the next verse is written, we have to say...

Thankiou!

. . . .

THANKIOU #93
TEAMWORK

There is no I in a team. Even though there are superstars that have amazing abilities and aptitudes to do a lot of things, it takes a group of people to accomplish great things. One player cannot win a championship, it takes the whole team; one person cannot run a business, it takes managers, employees, suppliers and clients to get it done. As in every relationship, it takes two people to make it work and last. When people work together towards the same goal and all cylinders fall in the right place, it deserves a big round of applause. And before we pick our next team, we have to say...

Thankiou!

. . . .

Countdowns 10, 9, 8, 7... 3, 2, 1. Every hour, minute and second counts toward reaching this anticipated moment. Waiting for a particular moment makes it desirable, intriguing and mysterious. We have no idea how something might turn out, but life gives us opportunities to expose the good and bad and make the ideal decision to achieve the expected goal. Countdowns are time bombs filled with expectations and goals; it's all about the amount of time we have left that makes everything feel so real. And before the countdown is over, we have to say...

Thankiou!

THANKIOU #95
RESTING AFTER A LONG DAY

Some days are longer than others, some are more hectic and some just run on automatic. For those days where we work extremely loooong hours, the best reward is resting. Taking off the shoes, tie, long sleeve shirt, socks and putting on pajamas is very rewarding. It's always a great moment when we just sit back with a cold drink, some relaxing music and just watch a movie while lying in bed. The only way it gets better is if that special person comes up in our dreams. And before a well deserve vacations, we have to say...

Thankiou!

. . . .

The scientific method of projects: think, create, plan and execute. Coming up with a new idea is always a wonderful beginning for something that might grow into a lifetime experience. When it comes to project development we have to remember Thomas Edison's saying: an idea without execution, is a hallucination. With that in mind, we cannot leave the idea floating around, we have to build it, create a short and long term plan and, most importantly, complete it. After months of hard work, we will see our baby become real and enjoy its benefits. And before a new project begins, we have to say…

Thankiou!

. . . .

WRITE AND DRAW YOUR
THANKIOU _____

_____

_____

_____

_____

_____

. . . .

TALKING ABOUT SOLUTIONS

Analysts, news reporters, and experts are always talking about the problems we all know we have in our lives. But when was the last time we sat with a cup of coffee and just talked about solutions? Deep down we all know the troubles and ways we can resolve them, but we get so caught up in the mumble jumble that we forget to do something about them. It's refreshing when solutions start coming up and the vibe transforms into a positive one. A change in our perspectives leads to a change in the collective mentality that leads to a change in reality. And before there are no more problems, we have to say...

Thankiou!

THANKIOU #98
THE LANGUAGE OF LOVE

Scientists say that body language accounts for 80% of the messages we send and receive and that what we actually say represents only 20%. Needless to say, non-verbal communication plays a huge role in people falling in love. This non-verbal happening occurs when two souls find each other and engage in a conversation impossible to explain. This language transcends oceans, nations and even cultures. In love, there are no boundaries to express what we feel inside but by living it every day. And before a translation is needed, we have to say...

Thankiou!

THANKIOU #99
CREATING SOMETHING BEAUTIFUL

It's a known fact that God created the beauty of life in just seven days. We have the same opportunity God had to create something beautiful every single day; it's one of his gifts to us. We can create a family, a business venture, a book, a career, positive campaigns, arts and craft, cookies, quotes, memories, among a million other things. The best part of creating something out of nothing is the collaboration between specific people at a certain time and place; it is destiny's map for us to trace. And before what we've created is ready, we have to say...

Thankiou!

. . . .

THANKIOUS
100-116

We live our whole life searching for that four-letter word: love. When we find it, the challenge changes and becomes a quest to express it in a tangible way. There are a million ways to utter this abstract sentiment: yelling of emotion, hugging, kissing passionately, writing, pouring the heart out, singing and talking about it. When the soul speaks, the world trembles. The moment its deep voice reaches the ear of its counterpart in another person, life makes the most sense and becomes extraordinary. And before the connection becomes endless, we have to say...

Thankiou!

THANKIOU #101
WHEN A FRIEND SUCCEEDS

There's an old saying that goes like this: friends are like stars, they come and go, but the ones who stay are the ones that glow. Those who keep on with us until our last breath, are the ones we can really call family. In each of their milestones, we get to celebrate like it's our own accomplishment. Big or small, successes are measured in ounces of happiness and hard work. And before the champagne pops, we have to say...

Thankiou!

. . . .

THANKIOU #102
FOR OUR ANCESTORS

In order to know the future, we shall look back at our history. We are who we are in large part because of our ancestors. They came to the world, then they cross the oceans and since we have been developing a gigantic family in 7 different continents. That's why, we have to be grateful for our parents and grandparents, but also for Jesus, Aristotle, Gandhi, Mother Theresa, MLK, among others. Our past can dictate how globalization can continue to evolve, and one day everything can change. And before the future comes, we have to say...

Thankiou!

· · · · · · · ·

BEING **THANKFUL** IS MORE THAN A WORD OR A SENTIMENT; IT'S A STATE OF MIND.

THE COUNTRY OF FIVE STARS

Christopher Columbus arrived at this country on his fourth and final voyage to the New World. Located in the center of Central America, this nation is filled with history from the Mayan civilization and Hernan Cortes to Francisco Morazán. It has a vast array of natural resources like fruits (bananas, coffee), rainforests, beaches and fauna (birds, reefs), but their most important asset is their people. It's incredible that in a relatively small and humble country we can find unique people that can share their hearts and change our lives forever. And before we cross paths again, we have to say...

Thankiou!

THANKIOU #104
IMAGINATION

Carl Sagan once said imagination will often carry us to worlds that never were, but without it we go nowhere. Imagination is the real sixth sense. We develop this unordinary sense as kids in the playground and we foster it as we grow up. Imagination land is a colorful, mind-boggling, fun and loving place full of adventures and dreams. When we imagine, we can feel the closeness to that special person we want to kiss, the revelation of an innovative idea or the triumphal entrance to a distant planet. And before we come back to Plant Earth, we have to say...

Thankiou!

Planning the future is preparing for the unknown. We have no idea what's in store for us, but we can be sure of what we want to be, do and have. Structuring our present is the key of a successful outlook. It's all about figuring out the elements that will surround our future selves in order to make the right decisions today. Planning is just one of the steps to accomplish what we most want in the long run. It's all about turning into our present, into that unique moment we have been waiting for. And before the future is the past, we have to say...

Thankiou!

THANKIOU #106
SURPRISING SOMEONE

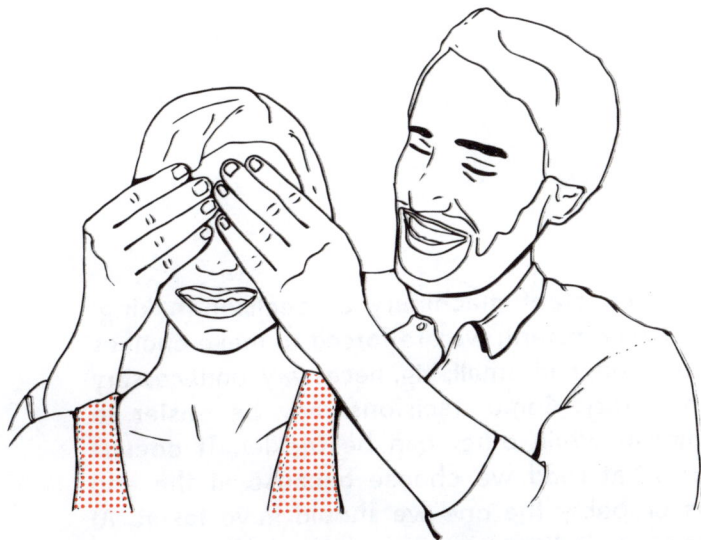

1, 2, 3, SURPRISE! The planning and the intrigue that leads up to the moment of the surprise is why we do it for. We have to arrange every little detail, involve key people and elaborate a well-constructed white lie. Hours, days and weeks can pass but when the moment comes and everything turns out the way we planned it: boom! The facial expressions, the yell and the smile are priceless. And before the next totally unexpected moment, we have to say...

Thankiou!

. . . .

Life is a constant machinery of decision-making. Almost every instant, we are forced to make choices that are good, bad, small, big, necessary, unnecessary or mandatory. Some decisions may be easier to accomplish while other can be trickier. It doesn't matter what road we choose because at the end it was probably the one we should have taken. At that moment in time, we are faced with the reality of our judgment and if we had it right, let's just smile in silence. And before the next decision, we have to say...

Thankiou!

THANKIOU #108
THE BUTTERFLY EFFECT

When butterflies arrive, it can only mean one thing: love is in the air. Upon their appearance, the sun shines brighter, the moon seems bigger, the stars glow intensely, every phone call becomes a smile, every message an exciting instant and every word exchange becomes everlasting. This effect turns our world upside down, literally. We don't eat, sleep well or think straight, but we have never felt more alive in our lives. It's the tipping point of the forever and ever. And before more butterflies arrive, we have to say...

Thankiou!

THANKIOU #109
FOR BEING MORE THAN HAPPY

Being happy is one thing, being more than happy is another. Throughout the day, a lot of things can have a positive effect on us, making us feel happy, but just one can make us feel more than that. To reach that next level, we have to reach for the stars, say what we truly feel and be responded equally. When it happens, enjoy the moment and smile. And before our cheeks start to hurt, we have to say...

Thankiou!

. . . .

Gratitude
is not only the greatest of virtues, but the parent of all others.

Cicero

There is always one friend that wants to bet on everything. Who's going to win the ball game? How is the movie going to end? Who's picking up a girl first? Who is going to marry first? Although bets can be somehow complicated and controversial, they give us a reason to stay one step ahead of the game, forecast the future with facts, become an expert at a certain topic and play with the odds. It doesn't matter who wins or lose, it's all about debating and challenging the mind. And before it's double or nothing, we have to say...

Thankiou!

THANKIOU #111
BUILDING CASTLES IN THE AIR

More than a fiction of our imagination, this castle is the explicit vision of everything we want out of life. The most important thing is to build the foundation. Once we have a strong foundation built in, communication, trust, understanding, simplicity, laughter, passion, and most importantly, love, the castle will start to become real. Many people might not understand it, but they don't have to. Castles are only meant for two people that want to share the same wonderful dream. And before the castle picks a landing place, we have to say...

Thankiou!

After a long and hard work day, all we want is to get home and take a well-deserved hot bath. When we start to unload everything we have on -wallets, shoes, socks, shirts, pants, belt, jewelry, jacket- it feels like all the stress from the day has also dropped. After getting everything off, the next step is to put some instrumental music, turn on an incense, put the shower in hot mode, turn the lights off and let the mind wander. This scene creates an unwinding ambiance full of peace and harmony. And before the next work day, we have to say...

Thankiou!

THANKIOU #113
WHEN OUR TEAM WINS

Nobody in this world enjoys losing. That's why, every time the team who we follow loses, it angers us and we feel disappointed. On the other hand, when the team plays beautifully and wins, it creates an overwhelming sense of completion and happiness in our lives. It doesn't matter if the game was won by 20 points or 1 point, a win is a win in any book. After a win, all we have to do is grab a drink, start celebrating and watch history in the making. And before the next game, we have to say...

Thankiou!

. . . .

The great Charlie Chaplin once declared that a day without laughter is a day wasted. We shall all find excuses -good or bad- to laugh and make our days worthwhile. When a joke, moment, story or situation is extremely funny, we laugh without barriers, without thinking what people might think of us and until it hurts deep in our stomachs. It's good to be alive. That feeling is more than a shortage of breath, it is happiness transformed into continuous chuckles and giggles. And before milk comes out of our noses, we have to say...

Thankiou!

THANKIOU #115
SITTING AT A PLAZA

Anything can happen just by sitting alone at a public space. There's always a bench next to a tree that allows us a relaxing and enjoyable time in between nature's glory. From time to time, a very colorful old man tells stories, birds sing in chorus, the wind splashes our faces with the scent of leaves, inspiration strikes vividly and everything around moves in a relaxation mode. When sitting in a plaza, we engage in very deep conversation with ourselves and put together plans for the rest of the day, and sometimes life. And before it starts raining, we have to say...

Thankiou!

. . . .

THANKIOU #116
RELIVING MEMORIES

For every moment we live, there is another moment to relive it. It could be hours, years or even decades from the time something occurs to the time we laugh and think about it again. Photographs, writings and videos are the usual keepers of life recollections. They can make any circumstance -happy or sad- an everlasting piece of history. The best memories are the ones we forget, but then a random picture remind us of that event and our soul feels splendid. And before we create the next memory, we have to say...

Thankiou!

. . . .

THANKIOUS
117-133

Over the course of our lives, the mind absorbs a lot of different things, concepts and information. Some will develop quickly into actions, other will stay in our minds forever, some will be forgotten and others will be transmitted to someone else. Sharing the understanding of a particular matter means that we have come a long way to master its ways. With that said, the receiving party is not just getting new information, it is receiving a part of our own personal history. And before we learn something new, we have to say...

Thankiou!

THANKIOU #118
RE-WATCHABLE MOVIES

How many times have we sat in front of the TV and watched the same movie? Probably a million times. There are certain movies we can watch, re-watch and are always entertaining. If we think about it, the reason we can review them so much is because they reminds us of a special moment, we first saw it with a special someone, the story is really our story or it just makes us feel good inside. Watching it today, tomorrow or in five years, the only certainty is that it will be time well spent. And before we watch another premier from 1999, we have to say...

Thankiou!

When we inaugurate something, it means a lot of hard work has been put together to create something from nothing. Blood, sweat and tears have been poured into a specific project or dream to make it become real. There are no words to describe a defining moment like this one, but there're a lot of people around us to be thankful for. It is the launch of a new phase in life, one full with an undefined path and adventures that will dictate the next years of our lives. And before the one year anniversary, we have to say...

Thankiou!

THANKIOU #120
SEEING SOMEONE AFTER A LONG TIME

Days, weeks, months and years can be in between of two persons getting to see each other. There is no precise reason as to why this happens, it just does. Work, adult responsibilities, illness and money issues can play a huge role in the reasons, but at the end it is the wiliness of everyone involved. Nevertheless, when the encounter occurs we can't stop talking, the smiles are endless, the questions are all over the place and it's almost like a miracle. And before life falls into place, we have to say...

Thankiou!

. . . .

Some mornings we will wake up -and for our surprise- find ourselves not feeling well. A fever, runny nose, cough or a tired body are some of the symptoms that take over our energies and smiles. In the mist of all the sickness, there's always a bright light that shines above all. By some kind of telepathy, our friends know that we are not feeling well and call us just to know how we are doing. A great man once said that there is always something good in the bad things. And before the next phone call, we have to say...

Thankiou!

. . . .

THANKIOU #122
SPORTSMANSHIP

Winning and losing at the same time is impossible, that's why sometimes we are going to be in the winning side and others on the losing end. The most important thing is to embrace losing with dignity, accept when the other team was better than us and keep playing the game with the same passion. Accepting defeat is the art absorbing knowledge that will later on be transformed into positive energy for us to be successful in the future. And before we take our hats off, we have to say...

Thankiou!

THANKIOU #123
UNEXPECTED HANGOUTS WITH FRIENDS

As a child, I learned that friends come and go, but the real ones always stay. Although that is real, we don't always see our friends with the frequency the relationship deserves. Nonetheless, when we go out to a restaurant, bar, club or mall, and unexpectedly run into one of our true friends it's unbelievable. The stars aligned in an impossible way for us to spend time together and nurture the bond. And before we run out of things to say, we have to say...

Thankiou!

. . . .

Make it a daily habit: every morning, open your eyes and say THANKIOU.

THANKIOU #124
FAMILY MEMBERS OVER 90 YEARS OLD

In the early 20th century, the average life expectancy was 31 years and by the start of the 21th century the average age was 72 years. What has changed? Western medicine has played a huge role, as well as, better eating habits. Not all of us will reach the average age and just a few will break the 90 years barrier. When a family member, grandparents or parents, almost reaches the three digits, it's indispensable to treasure every single moment. And before the next birthday, we have to say...

Thankiou!

THANKIOU #125
FALLING ASLEEP IN THE MIDDLE OF A CROWD

When exhaustion knocks on the door, there is no way to escape it; the only thing left is to fall asleep. The ideal place to take a nap is in a bed, but getting a sleepy head is something that can happen without notice and a bed could be out of reach. There are moments in which a couch, work chair, sofa at a hotel lobby, classroom desk or the back seat of a car can be superlative alternatives. Those fifteen minutes in which we take a nap in the middle of someplace crowded are unforgettable, especially if we don't feel ashamed. And before we wake up and everyone is looking at us, we have to say...

Thankiou!

. . . .

Thousands of games are played yearly in more than 8,000 different sports around the world. Only a small number of them are well known. Major sports -basketball, baseball, soccer, football and hockey- are played, followed and loved by a gigantic fan base that lives and dies for them. When a game is battled from beginning to end, played with passion and heart and the big plays are made by the hall of famers, they become classics. And before the next forever moment, we have to say...

Thankiou!

thankiou for...

THE KISS THAT NEVER HAPPENED

In love and lust, things rarely turn out as we would like them to be. We can go out with the girl we used to stare at school, but it doesn't mean we are going all the way. Lots of things have to align perfectly to get out of the friend zone and into the happily ever after. If we are unlucky enough to never kiss her, it's okay, life has another plan for us. And before we try to kiss her, we have to say...

Thankiou!

. . . .

THANKIOU #128
TREE HUGGERS

Mother Nature is a mother to us all and we should do everything we can to make her feel safe. Evolution and industrialization have done some terrible things to the environment over the years, and we have felt the fury of her power taking it back. We -human beings- are guests in this planet and shall not act in a disrespectful manner to her hospitality. As paladins of the world, tree huggers defend with their own lives, the beauty and miracle that God built in just seven days. And before we plant another tree, we have to say...

Thankiou!

THANKIOU #129
HEALTHY DEBATES

Debates are an exchange of points of views from very different people with diverse backgrounds and personalities. They can be very heated and controversial, and at the same time, respectful and full of understanding. When debates are intelligently dispute, they become an exchange of ideas. Critical thinking and open hearing sessions rule the day and make the path for a better-supported opinion. And before the next knotty verdict, we have to say...

Thankiou!

. . . .

THANKIOU #130
FREE TICKETS

Entertainment is part of our daily routine and almost every week there is an event we want to go. Costs can be an impairment for us to attain some events, but sometimes there are some friends that can make it happen. Concerts, expos, trade shows, food festivals, conferences and conventions can be an effective way to meet key people, do business, enjoy life pleasures and hang out, but when they are free, it elevates its satisfaction by a lot. And before the next free event, we have to say...

Thankiou!

THANKIOU #131
FULL MOON IN THE SKY

The night might be twelve hours of mystery and darkness, but once a month, we are blessed to have a glance of the gigantic ball of cheese that lights up the gloomy sky. Having a full moon in the night's sky is something that has inspired poets, singers and writers for generations. Its rays bleed romanticism and anticipate the start of new things to come. Life is full of obscure valleys, but a vivid moon can be the sun in our nights. And before the next full moon, we have to say...

Thankiou!

. . . .

THANKIOU #132
FORGOTTEN STUFF

At least once a year, we tend to do a deep cleaning of our rooms. We dig inside the closets, drawers, boxes and every corner looking for stuff we no longer need, items that can be donated and others that are to be relocated. Every once in a while we find little gems that we are not expecting like old photographs, love letters, old school toys, antique technology and cloth that doesn't fit anymore. It's like doing a scavenger hunt of our own lives without a map or compass. And before we find a dollar bill inside a pocket, we have to say...

Thankiou!

Love is a two-way street. To make it work, each of the persons involved has to give as much as they get. It's all about communication, trust and loyalty. The only ideal moment to argue about something is when the question of 'who loves whom the most?' comes up. The 'I love you' phrase becomes an argument point. Exchanging emotions in written, spoken or non-verbal ways is the equivalent of bartering with hearts, souls, hugs and kisses. And before exchanging love in a physical way, we have to say...

Thankiou!

THANKIOUS
134-147

Water is probably the most powerful and uncontrollable element known to man. The ocean is the laying place of their kingdom and glory. To show off its monumental force, water speaks to us through its waves, that's why they move vigorously, follow patterns and make sounds. Not everyone can decode what they are trying to tell us, but those who do come to understand a mysterious part of Mother Nature. And before we surf them, we have to say...

Thankiou!

· · · · · · · · ·

WHEN LEADERSHIP TERMS END

It's not really the end, it's the start of something else. When a term comes to the point of no return, it is a good moment to sit, think and relive. Looking back at all the things we have done during the course of our term is satisfying, fulfilling and graceful. In that time, we inspired people, created value for an organization, developed friendships and built a stronger self. At the end, we see the big picture with a heart full of memories. And before the next term starts, we have to say...

Thankiou!

THANKIOU #136
FOR WATCHING HOW THINGS ARE MADE

Buying and using products is one thing, but learning their story is another. Most products we consume on a daily basis are -most of the time- made in an unknown country, with machines we had no idea they existed and were done by a team of the most passionate people on the planet. In rare occasions, we have the unique opportunity to take an inside look at how things are done from the inside, understand their purposes and histories. It's like doing reverse engineering with a human touch. And before the next plant tour, we have to say...

Thankiou!

. . . .

THANKIOU #137
ADRENALINE RUSH

When the adrenal gland releases dopamine and endorphin, all our body gets hyped and our brains function in 'high' mode. It also acts as a natural painkiller and causes the muscles to perform at an increased rate. It's almost like having temporary superpowers. During this charge of energy, things are done quickly, efficiently, effectively and without fear. Getting this rushes from time to time is necessary in order to deal with certain situations in life. And before the next dash of power, we have to say...

Thankiou!

. . . .

THANKIOU #138
WHEN FRIENDS BECOME FAMILY

There are different kind of friends for different kind of topics, moments and situations. We all have a friend who enjoys talking about sports, other that we only call to hang out, others who understand our emotions, another just to talk about girls and some to do business with. Over our lifetime, we will have a lot of friends and acquaintances, but only a few -after a life altering experience- become our extended family. And before we add another chair to the Thanksgiving table, we have to say...

Thankiou!

THANKIOU #139
TAKING GRANDPARENTS FOR A STROLL

Life is a cycle. Grandparents used to take care of us when we were babies, but the formula is inverted when they are in their golden years. As a child, our grandparents took us to the park and school, twenty years into the future and it's us who are now taking them for coffee and to a doctor appointment. Moments like these are to be treasured more than when we were little because not all of them will live in our memories as vividly as the ones lived today. And before the next Sunday stroll, we have to say...

Thankiou!

. . . .

THANKIOU #140
WAKING UP FEELING A LOT BETTER

The fever is gone, the runny nose stopped and the tired body feels like a rejuvenated one. Life is beautiful again: colors seem brighter, the air feels refresher, birds sing with the wind and food tastes like heaven. It's like waking up in a parallel universe where everything seems like it's filled with sugar, spice and everything nice. There are no words to describe how everything around us smiles and exfoliates love. And before the next time we survive an infection, we have to say...

Thankiou!

It is not happy people who are **thankful**. It is **thankful** people that are happy.

Unknown

Time is the only thing that we can't get back. Life is a continuum of time and space which we all need to spend in the wisest way. The weird thing about time is that it moves at different speeds varying the situations. For example, when we are doing an uncomfortable task it goes by slowly, but when we are having fun, doing something we love goes really fast. Abraham Lincoln said the best thing about the future is that it comes one day at a time. And before we realize the time we have lost, we have to say...

Thankiou!

THANKIOU #142
TV NIGHT WITH FAMILY

Normally, Saturday is a day to dress up, go out and have some fun. But fun doesn't mean that we cannot spend the whole night inside the house watching regularly programmed TV with close family. One of the best things about staying at home is when our mom starts bringing different kinds of snacks every few minutes and by the end of the night we are stuffed with candy, juice, ice cream, popcorn, etc. Every time something interesting comes up in the TV, it sparks a deep friendly ponder that's priceless. And before the next TV program starts, we have to say...

Thankiou!

For centuries, we have developed and perfected the process of distilling certain types of liquids. Rum, whiskey and vodka have been made to satisfy and quench the thirst of everyone. More than something to drink and match with food, distilled spirits are art in a bottle. These spirits are blended and aged for years and years in order to reach the precise taste and flavor needed to create good times. And before the next sip, we have to say...

Thankiou!

. . . .

THANKIOU #144
IMPROVISED RADIO SHOWS

When a group of friends and acquaintances get together to talk, drink and have a good time, it's totally normal to engage in heated debates. Some of the topics that usually are brought to the table are political endeavors, world problems and sports rivalries. In a respected discussion, ideas and well-thought points of view are exchanged making the surrounding feel like a live radio talk show; the only thing missing are the commercials. And before we are contacted by a national radio station, we have to say...

Thankiou!

. . . .

There are some days we wake up having a particular desire for something. All day long we talk and think about it and the only way to get it out of our heads is to eat it. At certain points of the day, we find ourselves drooling about the restaurant or food joint that serves the best pizza, hamburger, fried chicken, ice cream or juicy steak. When the time comes and we actually satisfy that craving, it's almost orgasmic. The world can end at that precise moment and it will all be worth it. And before the next hankering, we have to say...

Thankiou!

THANKIOU #146
MANAGING DIFFICULT SITUATIONS

Life has its bad, good, hard, easy, difficult, awesome, challenging, confusing, bright and complicated moments. There are a lot of times that life will give us reasons to smile, be happy and enjoy every minute of it, but from time to time, life will present to us with sad, problematic and inexplicable situations that need to be fixed. Not everything will go as planned or desired but with the help of friends, family and past life experiences we can -and will- manage them until everything is okay in the world again. And before the next terrible, horrible, no good, very bad day, we have to say...

Thankiou!

. . . .

THANKIOU #147
WHEN EVERYONE HAS FUN

When a group of people gets together for a social event or some kind of gathering there is one implicit goal: to have fun. It's nearly impossible to meet everyone's expectations, but everything that's needed to get done in order to accomplish it, it's done. Sometimes a funny and dynamic conference or a little alcohol can be the spark plug to an unforgettable experience. At the end, when everyone is smiling and getting along, it means a good time was broad to life. And before the next memorable experience, we have to say...

Thankiou!

THANKIOUS
148-167

THANKIOU #148
WHEN A FRIEND'S MOM COOKS

If a plate of food it's given to us be a friend's mom, we can't say no; it's a rule. After that, we just need to get prepared to be stuffed with some native dish in excessive quantities. Most of the times the food is delicious, out of this world and although we might be full, we just can't stop eating. Usually, it's unexpected to be served food at a friend's house, but when it happens the belly will be filled with the secret ingredient in every mom's kitchen: love. And before the dessert comes, we have to say...

Thankiou!

THANKIOU #149
DAYDREAMING

When the feeling of missing someone is much bigger than what we can handle, we start imagining stuff. Daydreaming resides in a completely different world where all our desires come alive in our minds. As we enter that world, everything seems perfect and fits into our hearts in the right way. It may not be real, but it is as real as it gets. And before we start confusing our reality with our dreams, we have to say...

Thankiou!

. . . .

The night has an inexplicable force that drives our inner self to express thoughts and feelings in a beautiful way. When two people speak -and the lights are out- it feels like the world is empty and they are the only ones left. This factor brings out the best of us because the mind is at ease and the body relaxed; it's all about the heart and soul speaking out. Not even tiredness can keep us from talking long hours. When the conversation is meaningful, nothing else matters. And before the sun is up, we have to say...

Thankiou!

Let us rise up and
be thankful,
for if we didn't
learn a lot today,
at least we learned a little,
at least we didn't got sick,
at least we didn't die;
so let us all
be thankful.

Buddha

CLOTHES WITH STORIES

Going shopping can be an enjoyable but stressful adventure. Out of necessity we buy clothes, shoes and accessories that we like, are in style and fit us. We wear them on normal days, special occasions and sometimes to impress. Some of them live through our most remarkable moments in life, and when we wear them again, they take us back. It's a sad day when we have to replace them with new ones because in our hearts it's the end of an era. And before we enter the next store, we have to say...

Thankiou!

THANKIOU #152
LOOKING AND FINDING

Through our life, we spend most of the time searching for something: love, clothes, stuff, friends, adventures, jobs, among others. Not every time we are lucky enough to get it the easy way or to find it at all, but when we do, it gives us a sense of completion and closure. The truth is that finding it is not the real goal, it is the journey what we are really aiming for. On that unknown path, life becomes the professor and teach us the why, how and what, of everything we are missing. And before we find something amazing, we have to say...

Thankiou!

WRITE AND DRAW YOUR
THANKIOU _____

THANKIOU #153
SURVIVING SLEEPY DAYS

The eternal battle between man and the blanket. There are some days when it's almost impossible to get out of bed. Why? The mind might be awake, but the body is still in nirvana. There are a lot of reasons that can make us sleepy throughout the day: late-night coffee, stress, insomnia, partying, work, muse, etc. In reality, there is nothing bad about going to bed late, it's the sleep hangover the very next day what makes us almost regret our late-night excess. Somehow we have to fight sleep and figure out how to keep up with our daily tasks, but it's a battle not always won. And before we fall asleep in our work table, we have to say...

Thankiou!

. . . .

There are millions and millions of things in the world to like, dislike, love and hate. Our DNA, personality and family learning's will dictate our ways in every aspect of our lives. As human beings, we are totally different from one another and interests will vary most of the times, but when they coincide, it's special. Having similar interests is a favorable sign of great things to come. And before we fall in love with a new interest, we have to say...

Thankiou!

THANKIOU #155
COMMUNAL LUNCH

Our behavior is the result of hundreds and hundreds of generations that precede us. History shows that we have not had a quick evolution, we have just evolved to a more complicated human being than 2,000 years ago. As the old saying goes, some things never change and it is perfectly exemplified in the way we eat in groups. Jesus Last Supper was an example of sharing food between friends and family -and today- we are still celebrating eating rituals among the ones we most appreciate. And before the check arrives, we have to say...

Thankiou!

THANKIOU #156
CONVERSATIONS THAT WILL CHANGE THE WORLD

Once in a while, we find ourselves with a special person sipping coffee or tea and having a rational discussion about solutions to change the way we live. During this conversations problems arise, questions begin to swirl around and ideas find their way around the table. Talking and planning are part of the game, but in order to create positive change and impact the lives of many, we have to put words into action. And before the political campaign starts, we have to say...

Thankiou!

THANKIOU #157
WHEN POLITICIANS ACTUALLY DO SOMETHING

Politicians have bad fame for talking way too much and not delivering. Those individuals are public servants elected by the people and for the people. When the moment comes and the politician shuts up and stands up to do the right thing, purposes are fulfilled. Every step forward they take, in order to create things that matter and help the people, the country starts glowing in a different way. And before the next elections, we have to say...

Thankiou!

. . . .

We all have a friend from a different cultural background. Intrigued by the traditions and customs of this comrade, a friendly questionnaire commences in order to understand his past. Without a doubt, the first thing we can all do to comprehend the culture is to taste its gastronomy. The first scoop of a funky, bizarre and tasty dish makes us think about the hundreds of generations that came before us and the hundreds that will follow, who have and will taste this piece of history. And before the next tasting, we have to say...

Thankiou!

THANKIOU #159
WHEN KIDS IMITATE GOOD THINGS

Leading by example is one of the most honorable and encouraging sayings ever been told. If we live by it, we can inspire hundreds, thousands and sometimes millions of people to do amazing things for a greater good. It's even more meaningful when a kid follows our footsteps and starts imitating our laughter, gestures, words and actions. Becoming a positive influence and being a role model is a way to change the course of the future, for the better. And before kids inspire the next generation, we have to say...

Thankiou!

. . . .

THANKIOU #160
ONCE IN A LIFETIME OPPORTUNITIES

God works in mysterious ways. There are things that happen for reasons we don't even understand and in the most peculiar circumstances. When we least expect it BOOM, a once in a lifetime opportunity falls right in our laps. Unbelievably, this break that life is giving us is no joke and thereby we have to seize it -as fast as we can- and make it feasible. Not every day we can be at the right time in the right moment with the right people. And before the stars align again, we have to say...

Thankiou!

GRATITUDE IS THE ESSENCE OF A ★HAPPY LIFE★

Everyone has a story to tell. Those stories are a composition of lived experiences combined with learning's and emotions. As life plays out, we can only reminiscence these moments and take the best of them to inspire others to do the right thing in the right way; not because we already did it, but because it is our duty as responsible citizens. We can try a thousand times with a lot of people, but it only takes one to change the world. And before a new advice, we have to say...

Thankiou!

THANKIOU #162
THE FIRST DAY OF SCHOOL SENSATION

As kids, at least once every year, we had the most innocent and exiting celebration: the first day of school. This day was full of new adventures and people, unknown happenings and brand new stuff to try on. Getting ready for this moment is probably one of the best memories of being a child: buying new clothes and shoes, getting the book bag ready, wrapping up the notebooks and daydreaming about seeing again the girl we liked. And before anxiety let us fall asleep, we have to say...

Thankiou!

. . . .

THANKIOU #163
WHEN EVERYTHING IS PERFECT

Life is a combination of good, bad and so-so moments, but every now and then a perfect moment knocks on the door. In other for such a moment to arise, everything has to come together: the weather, the music, the smells, the girl, the time and place. We have to be very wary of them because when they come, the only way to fuel and prolong them is with faith, passion and love. And before we return to reality, we have to say...

Thankiou!

. . . .

THANKIOU #164
MULTIPLE BIRTHDAYS IN ONE DAY

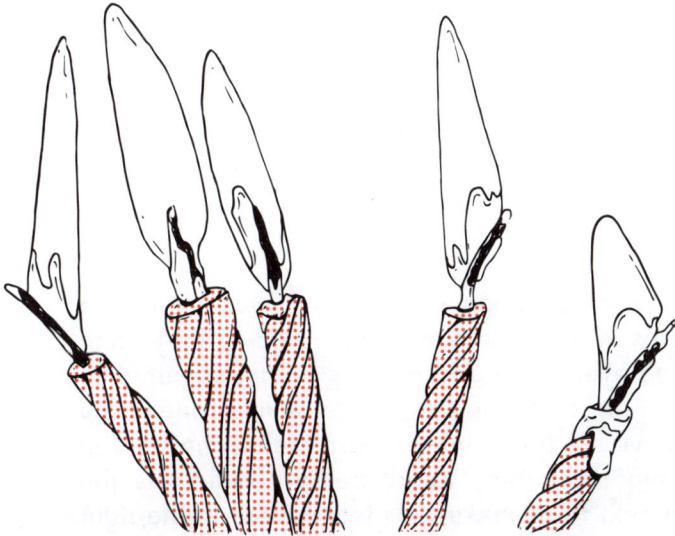

Year after year, there is one day that is more special than any of the others. This day marks the beginning of our mortal stories and is a cause for celebration. Birthdays are a great excuse for cake, gifts and family gathering to party like there is no tomorrow. The year has only 365 days and, Itherefore, some friends' birthdays will coincide, duplicating the fun, parties and joy. And before the next birthday party, we have to say...

Thankiou!

. . . .

THANKIOU #165
THE MIDDLE OF NOWHERE

Once every blue moon, we open our eyes just to find ourselves in the middle of nowhere. This interjection is where everything and nothing comes together to form the most amazing sight. We have no idea how or why we are there, but it doesn't really matter. The most important thing about being nowhere is the person next to us making us feel we are in the right place. And before we go back home, we have to say...

Thankiou!

THANKIOU #166
THE BEST FEELING OF THE WORLD

Millions and millions of poems and songs have been written and sung about this four-letter word. Without a doubt, it's the only thing in which we should exceed. It is more than an abstract emotion, it is the look in our eyes and the taste in someone else lips. When two people feel their heart pounding in an uncontrollable way and the need to be together, we know we are in love. And before our next encounter, we have to say...

Thankiou!

. . . .

We live and we die, that life's first rule. While we might not take money or material stuff to the afterlife, one thing that will forever be kept in our hearts are the moments we lived. A great thing to do after living something memorable is to remember it and talk about it with the ones we treasure the most. If we describe them with a lot of details we can feel the chills and thrills of the past moment. And before the déjà vu start coming, we have to say...

Thankiou!

. . . .

THANKIOUS
168-188

When destiny does its magic, miraculous things can happen for two people to meet. It's easy to notice that someone is our one and only, the hard part is to cross paths with them. Soul mates can be distinguished in the similarities and the differences that play roles in each other's life. For example: thinking and acting the same way, quoting the same philosophers, having the same tastes, being equally crazy, sharing dreams and feeling the same way towards love and life. And before the world is not big enough, we have to say...

Thankiou!

THANKIOU #169
SINGING ON THE PHONE

Picking up the phone, calling someone and starting to sing for no reason at all is wonderful. This crazy performance will put the biggest smile on the other person's face and will initiate a conversation on a positive vibe. It's a great way to surprise someone we love and at the same time express our feelings in a melodic tone. The important thing is to do it while holding on to the phone as if it were a microphone. And before the world premiere of our solo hit, we have to say...

Thankiou!

More refreshing than a pink lemonade on a hot summer day. Meeting people who see the world in the same crazy and optimistic way as we do is energizing. We get pumped up just to know that we can build and grow ideas that can change the social paradigm of the country we live in. The first step is to join forces and sooner than later, we will watch everything growing and leading in the right direction. And before the next big thing is created, we have to say...

Thankiou!

THANKIOU #171
FROZEN YOGURT

It's not quite ice cream nor yogurt; it's frogurt. A delicious, nutritious, low fat, real fruit, gluten-free, high in fiber, healthy, high in vitamin C, non-dairy, made with real fruit, probiotic and guilt-free frozen dessert. This yummy delight is all we need to live a strong and active lifestyle. So next time we have a desert menu with all kind of cheesecakes, let do the right thing and take the frozen yogurt route. And before the next guilt-free moment, we have to say...

Thankiou!

. . . .

Every once in a while there is one day in which we are eternally tired. We get up just to fall asleep once again; it's a never-ending vicious circle. We sleep so much during the day that our energy level is like one from someone who spent the whole day working hard or playing sports. Sleeping all day long is like taking the body and mind to a one-day compressed mini vacation to release the daily life stress. And before it's time to go to bed again, we have to say...

Thankiou!

. . . .

THANKIOU #173
BEING IN LOVE

The greatest feeling in the whole world is to find yourself in another person's soul. Being in love is more than a physical attraction that captivates us, it is giving away our fears, sharing our secrets and soaking in the history of someone else. It is an abstract idea until we hear the most magical words, touch the most electrifying hands, kiss the tenderest lips, see the heart pounding in an abnormal rhythm and smell that love is really in the air. And before everything is more perfect than perfection, we have to say...

Thankiou!

THANKIOU #174
JOKING AROUND WITH A FRIEND

All work and no play makes Jack a dull boy, is a famous movie phrase that has truth all over it. Not everything has to be about work, sometimes we have to let it out, joke, laugh and simply let it flow. With a childhood friend is easier to joke around because there is a long history of moments that were funny, sad and embarrassing, so the jokes come out easily. They say laughter is a great medicine, but doing it with a friend is the stairway to heaven. And before the next knockout joke, we have to say...

Thankiou!

I CAN NO OTHER ANSWER MAKE BUT THANKS AND THANKS, AND EVER THANKS

William Shakespeare

THANKIOU #175
WHEN MOM CLEANS OUR APARTMENT

As a child, we always saw mom doing the dishes, mopping the floors, dry cleaning the clothes, taking out the trash and folding the sheets. As time passed, she incorporated us in the daily tasks to help unload some of the work and prepare us for the future. As adults, most of us are independent and maintain the house fresh, but when our mom stays at our place she can't help it and cleans everything, even though it's already clean. And before her next visit, we have to say...

Thankiou!

THANKIOU #176
WHEN THINGS TURN BETTER THAN EXPECTED

We work hard to create and develop things from scratch, but life isn't as glamorous as TV shows. In order to get it right, a plan has to be crafted, a team assembled, the execution has to be in order and luck has to be present. Although we might have all the ingredients to be successful in a particular thing, we have no idea what the future has in place for us. When things turn better than projected and expectations are exceeded, we know we were blessed by the Big Guy in the Sky. And before the stress levels go down and the smiles appear, we have to say...

Thankiou!

. . . .

THANKIOU #177
BEING AMAZED BY A STRANGER

Each day has a happy moment, a sad moment, an exciting moment, an unbelievable moment and a miraculous moment. As life teaches us, everything happens for a reason and the people we meet are part of our life for a particular and sometimes odd motive. Every now and then, a complete stranger says or does something that amazes us and changes everything we believe in or gives us a reason to believe in something else. And before the next strange encounter with a stranger takes place, we have to say...

Thankiou!

. . . .

THANKIOU #178
SANDWICHES

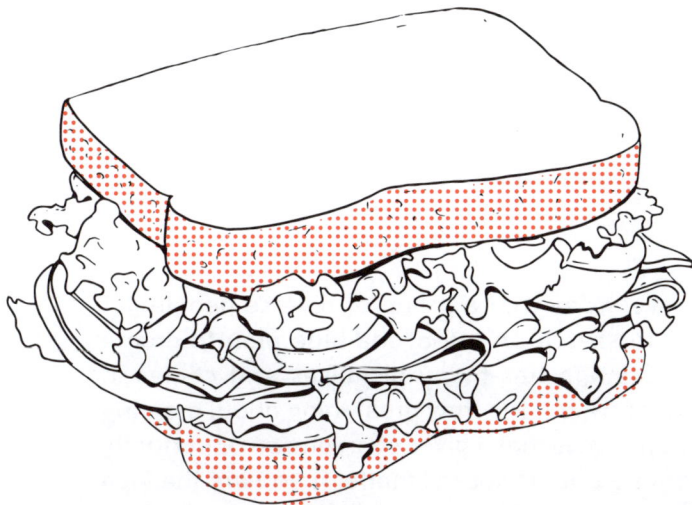

Fast. Portable. Inexpensive meal. Sandwich origins can be traced back hundreds of years. The awesome thing about them is that they are very easy to assemble and the variations are endless. There is a variety of bread types, spreads, meats, vegetables, fruits, sauces and cooking techniques to choose from. The end product of all the ingredients -mixed as we wish- will create a unique bread wrapped piece of deliciousness. The cherry on top of it is that we can eat them as breakfast, lunch, dinner or snack. And before we eat it completely, we have to say...

Thankiou!

· · · · · · · ·

THANKIOU #179
CREATING A POSITIVE CHANGE

It's not every day that a group of diverse people get together to sketch an out-of-the-blue plan to create change. Change has many disguises and comes in different forms, but the truly great thing about creating positive change is that it gives everyone an opportunity for a better world. It doesn't matter if you are the idea man, the executor, the special collaborator, a one-time volunteer or a diehard change maker. To create a positive revolution we have to act more and talk less. And before the world is a better place for everyone, we have to say...

Thankiou!

THANKIOU #180
GROWING UP

When we realize that our usual conversations with friends changed from fun to serious, there is something unusual happening. We all have stories that start with late night parties, meeting people at random places, unplanned road trips and school occurrences. Time passes so fast that those stories become less wild and turn into brunch Sundays, weddings, couple stuff, farmers markets and work issues. At that moment, we realized that we are no longer teenagers and we have all grown up. And before we notice our first gray hair, we have to say...

Thankiou!

What is the purpose of life? What is my purpose? What am I doing in this time and place? If I wake up tomorrow, will I be doing what I am doing today? Will I ever fulfill my dreams? What is my passion? What do I absolutely love in life? When will I find love? Could I have a better job, house or car? Am I happy? How happy? What would be my legacy? Will people remember my name? And before we have all the answers, we have to say...

Thankiou!

Today
I'm
THANKFUL
for
yesterday,
tomorrow
I will be
THANKFUL
for
today
and someday,
I will be
THANKFUL
for
tomorrow.

Oscar Wilde said that the only good thing to do with good advice is to pass it on; it is never of any use to oneself. With that in mind, it is our duty as solidarity human beings to help our brothers and sisters with good advice that they can later apply in their daily lives, helping them to achieve anything. This guidance can be instrumental in the decision-making process of someone's dreams or goals. And before our next judgment call, we have to say...

Thankiou!

THANKIOU #183
BROWSING THROUGH
OLD PICTURES

They only thing we take to the next life is the memories of what we lived and some of them are immortalized in beautiful full-color photos. Photos say a million things and never lie. They just take us from one good moment to the next without ever reminding us of the hard and sad times. When browsing through them we have to be careful that our faces don't get wrinkled with all the smiling. And before we reminiscence a little more, we have to say...

Thankiou!

What to do with it? We turn it into a game room, office, guest room or huge walking closet. The possibilities are endless and the matchmaking is challenging, but if we are ready for the task, the room will live to our expectations. After picking the colors, theme and furniture it's up to the imagination to put the pieces together and create a masterpiece. And before the room is ready, we have to say…

Thankiou!

THANKIOU #185
THE SMELL OF RAIN

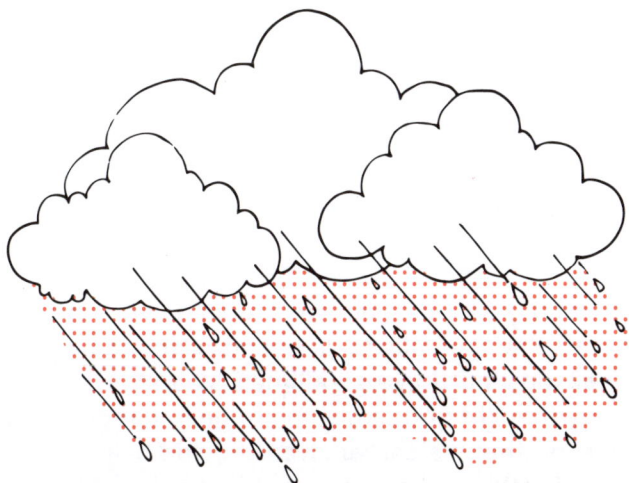

We feel the cold breeze, we see the gray skies and we know it's coming. But before the skies rinse our lands, it expels an invigorating aroma full of emotions and revelations. A smell that brings back the good old days, the feeling of coziness, the comfort of our beds and the desire of a hot steamy bowl of homemade soup. This is the perfect scenery for Mother Earth to perfume the environment with the fragrance of rain and the harmony of dripping water. And before it stops raining, we have to say...

Thankiou!

We can be as busy as a bee, but we should never skip a call. When someone calls us is because, for some unknown reason, the Universe aligned in a strange way and they thought of us. They might be in danger, have a question that we can answer, provide help in a particular situation or have good news to share. It doesn't matter the motive, it's always good to hear the ringing sound followed by a simple 'hello'. And before picking up the next call, we have to say...

Thankiou!

THANKIOU #187
NAILING THE PRESENTATION

We spent our whole life's preparing for big memorable moments that will probably make history. From time to time, life puts a diversity of challenges to test our learning skills and developed abilities. It is our job to always give 110% and pour our heart on it. If we spell out passion in every word, gesture and emotion we send out of our mind and body, we are without a doubt, nailing every presentation, exam and assessment they put in our way. And before the next defying moment, we have to say...

Thankiou!

Cars have become an essential part of our lives. The way the city infrastructure has been built forces us to drive an automobile from destination to destination. In our daily routine, this vehicle is so significant that when it breaks down, our whole life is messed up. Some of us are no experts in car engineering and are willing to pay any kind of money for it to get fixed in order to be back on the road as soon as possible. And before the next car maintenance, we have to say...

Thankiou!

. . . .

THANKIOUS
189-202

We are not all experts at sports. Some games are more sophisticated, strategic or need a lot of physical endurance to play them the right way, others just need a little effort to make them fun and playful. In bowling, we just need to throw the ball as straight as possible to hit some pins. It would be great to play like a pro and strike them all, but for us amateurs a spare (hitting them all in two turns) might just do the trick. And before we do the Flintstones bowling dance, we have to say...

Thankiou!

THANKIOU #190
THE RIGHT COLOR

There are thousands of colors in the Universe to choose from. Each one of them can set the mood for any particular situation. Matchmaking colors with shapes and things can convert an empty space into a livable vivid environment. Some colors make us hungry, depressed, hyper, alive and others set the tone for a romantic moment. It's up to us to pick the right color to create an atmosphere that makes our imagination fly away. And before the palette of colors is harmonized, we have to say...

Thankiou!

. . . .

DELEGATING TASKS

As leaders we cannot do it all, it's impossible. The best feature a leader should have is the ability to understand its team and how each of them can produce and contribute in the most efficient manner. When things need to get done in order to create or develop a project, it's about matchmaking between tasks and people. After that happens we just macro manage, do some fine tuning and enjoy the fruits of every single thing being done. And before the next project, we have to say...

Thankiou!

THANKIOU #192
GOLF CARTS

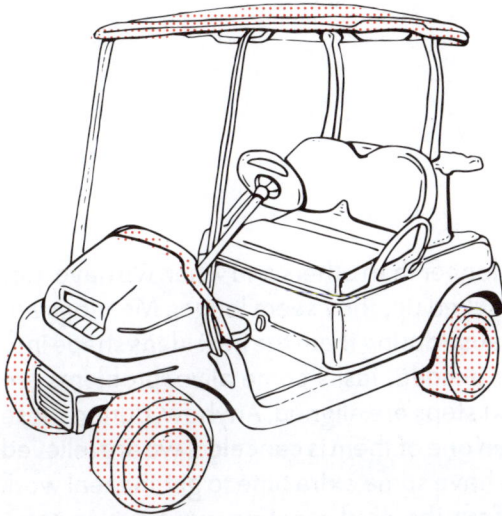

Don't we all wish to ride a golf cart at least once in our lifetime? They are just as fun as they look: miniature, with a hint of summer, picture perfect with a mojito and they sound like something from a futuristic movie. Golf carts are simply go-carts for adults. They are more than just for playing golf, we can use them as a transportation method inside access control residences, to do nearby chores, ride for fun in a big park, security services, valet parking and as a gift to the best dad in the world. And before the next golf cart adventure, we have to say...

Thankiou!

. . . .

Some days are longer than others and when we have a lot of meetings stacked up, they seem longer. Meetings are necessary because during them the best ideas shape Into reality, work is divided, tasks come alive, problems are solved and next steps are aligned. Anyhow, during these long days, when one of them is canceled, we are relieved and happy we have some extra time to get the real work done. And before the next meeting, we have to say...

Thankiou!

THANKIOU #194
WHEN A FRIEND TAKES US TO THE AIRPORT

When someone takes us to the airport and the sun is still hiding, we know he is someone who cares. Not everyone wakes up at 3:00 am to drive all the way to an airport when he is not the one going on the trip. Although he might not be joining us, he's still an important part of the whole experience and we will definitely reciprocate the gesture when his vacation time comes. And before the plane takes off, we have to say...

Thankiou!

. . . .

Problem-solving is a skill developed through tough life experiences. This power is employed almost every single day in our lives, sometimes in more urgent or complicated ways than others. In order to turn a problem into a solution, we have to: stay calm, evaluate all the possibilities, never think negatively and take action without holding our breath. Once tribulations are cracked, vanished and forgotten, life is good again. And before a plan B is needed, we have to say...

Thankiou!

GRATITUDE

**is said
to be the
memory of
the heart.**

THANKIOU #196
WHEN THE PAST TRANSLATES INTO THE FUTURE

In order to create something meaningful in life, we have to plant the seeds, nurture them and guide them through it all. Sometimes months and years can pass and we are not able to see the outcome of everything we started to build. But one day, all the pieces fall together and we see the big beautiful picture, and it's more than we could have ever imagined. And before the next seed germinates, we have to say...

Thankiou!

. . . .

THANKIOU #197
FANTASIZING MOMENTS

In the night we have dreams and nightmares and by day we daydream and fantasize. Dreams happen when we are alone, asleep and spaced out, but fantasizing occurs when two people share a moment in their dreams. They talk about it, join forces, finished each other's thoughts and create a memory that only lives in their imaginations. The only thing missing when we fantasize is for it to become real. And before it becomes a reality, we have to say...

Thankiou!

. . . .

THANKIOU #198
LIVING WITHOUT AN AGENDA

Even though we might have to plan, certain things in life should be left to play out alone. This happens when we get tired of planning and strategizing our every move. They might turn out for the better or worse, but the waiting kills us. In order to skip that step and anxiety, it is better to let everything flow without an agenda and hope for the best. And before the next unplanned moment, we have to say...

Thankiou!

. . . .

THANKIOU #199
LIFE CHANGING BOOKS

For every couple books we read, one is always a game changer. We know it's special because from the moment we read the first lines we are hooked. Then, at the middle of every chapter we have to stop to laugh, think, reflect and get ready for more. It's like every word speaks our own unique language and understands where we come from, how we think and where we want to be. The final words reflect on our own life and gives us new pages to start fresh. And before we finish reading the book, we have to say...

Thankiou!

. . . .

THANKIOU #200
VACATION AFTER VACATIONS

We spend all year long planning this magazine-like vacations and when they finally arrive, we have no time to waste. There is so much to do that waking up early is a must, walking a lot is a rule, trying to see everything Is the objective and going to bed late at night is inevitable. After we reach the end of the trip, we are exhausted and not ready to go back home. All we want is to take some days off to relax and sleep. And before we go back to reality, we have to say...

Thankiou!

THANKIOU #201
DID YOU KNOW?

Did you know that NASA is developing 3D printed pizzas for astronauts? Did you know that Queen Elizabeth served as a mechanic in WWII? Did you know that cherries can cause cancer cells to kill themselves? Did you know that the Statue of Liberty was originally meant to be in Egypt? Did you know that if the human eye was a digital camera, it would have 576 megapixels? Did you know that honey is the only food that does not rot and it can remain edible for 3,000 years? And before we learn something new, we have to say...

Thankiou!

Almost every month, there is one weekend that is longer that the others. We all wait for Fridays to arrive in order to get a break from the routine, relax and just forget about work. But in that particular one-in-a-month long weekend, the planning is better thought and the adventures become more complicated, interesting and enjoyable that usual. And before it's Tuesday, we have to say...

Thankiou!

THANKIOUS
203-216

THE PLACES WE HAVE BEEN

248,752 cities. 196 countries. 7 continents. 1 moon. There are a lot of places and just one life to get to know them all. Several of us are lucky enough to visit a few of them during our lifespan and every visited place becomes a treasured experience. We meet new people, learn about their cultures, try to understand their languages, are amazed by their gastronomy and admire their landmarks. In pictures, we frame these memories and share the colorful stories for years to come. And before our next trip, we have to say...

Thankiou!

. . . .

THANKIOU #204
SMELLS THAT BRING BACK MEMORIES

Randomly, we pass through some place or between a group of people and a particular scent caught our attention. It could be the perfume that our mom used to use when we were kids, the odor of a new trading cards deck, the freshness of a school morning, our grandpa's cologne or the aroma of some adored house. When the brain detects it, we have to stop, look at the horizon and smile for a while. It's a smell that brings back the good old days. And before the next stinky sparkle, we have to say...

Thankiou!

CANDLES FOR MEN

History tells that candles originated in China around 200 BC. They were used as a way to keep time but today it has more than one use, for example, illumination, aesthetic value, scent, heat and religious purposes. Candles have been directly related to women and their scents have been developed to their liking, leaving men in limbo. Things have changed and now we can find candles developed with scents such as tobacco, cigars, beer, gun powder, bacon, stainless steel and campfire. Nothing is as manly as the smell of fresh cut grass to make us sit back and relax. And before the man candle melts down, we have to say...

Thankiou!

THANKIOU #206
TRAIN RIDES

At some point in time, every child dreams of riding or driving a train. The first time we get to ride them is probably at the state fair, amusement park or some little local park. Riding in the big ones comes later in life. The NYC subway system, Amtrak or anyone in Europe is a luxury that brings the inner child in us again. When we actually get inside, it's an adventure of its own. Hearing the traction, the horn and walking through the narrow hallways that takes us from one cart to the other, it's an exceptional experience. Without a doubt, trains are the most fun way to get from point A to point B. And before the next "choo choo" sound, we have to say...

Thankiou!

. . . .

Sports are more than a competitive physical activity played in different scenarios, with a variety of artifacts and rules. Games are played off the court with other players that are not on the team, called fans. These aficionados become the singing voice and die-hard devotees of the team and players. Often, fans engage in very heated debates about who's going to win or lose, who's better, controversial plays and trades. These arguments are what maintain things interesting and make us come for more. And before we have a radio show to debate, we have to say...

Thankiou!

THANKIOU #208
SONGS THAT UNDERSTAND US

Songwriters have a special way of communicating with the world's beating heart. In it, they extract all accumulated emotions and decode them into black and white ink. As if it wasn't enough, those written words are then converted into the language of music. The final result is a masterpiece of sentiments that enter our bodies through our ears as a beautifully constructed sound. More often than we know, the song relates to our moods and thoughts; as if they were written for us. And before the song is over, we have to say...

Thankiou!

JOKES BETWEEN FRIENDS

Lots of things are bound to happen in the span of any friendship. From out of this world experiences to near death ones to funny or sad, anything is possible. Jokes tend to stands the test of time. They are born from a humorous situation that only a handful lived and understand. Time and time again they are brought up, remembered and told just for the fun of it. The greatest thing about them is that they never get old and everyone has a blast just by hearing it for the thousand time. And before the joke is told again, we have to say...

Thankiou!

THANK
YOU

GRAZIE
NGIYABONGA
Efharisto
DANK U
OBRIGADO
謝謝
ありがとう
TACK
DIOLCH
GRACIAS
ありがとう
MERCI
DANKE

Around the year 1873, jeans were invented by a man named Levi Strauss and were originally designed for cowboys. It wasn't until the 1950s that jeans became popular, especially among teenagers. This blue pants look good on everyone and are available in all sizes. The best part is that they match with every piece of cloth we own. Jeans make our world a little easier in the morning and less stressful when the dress code is tricky. And before they go out of style, we have to say...

Thankiou!

THANKIOU #211
CHILDHOOD DRAWINGS

When we were kids the world felt like a gigantic place full of colors, people and places. Every time something caught our attention we ran towards our special notebook to draw it like there was nothing more important around us. Hours were spent perfecting the sketch and coloring without leaving the borders. After completion, we proudly called our parents to show them the work of art and they'd hang it on the refrigerator door for everyone to see it. And before all our childhood memories come to our minds, we have to say...

Thankiou!

. . . .

Wanting and waiting to get mail every now and then is proof that human beings want to be part of something bigger. Having correspondence delivered to our homes means that someone out there thought about us and made us of part of their lives. Letters have been written by generations before us and will perpetuate into the future. This is the way the world communicates from north to south and from east to west. It is a special coded language only our species understands. And before the next post office visit, we have to say...

Thankiou!

THANKIOU #213
THE LAW OF ATTRACTION

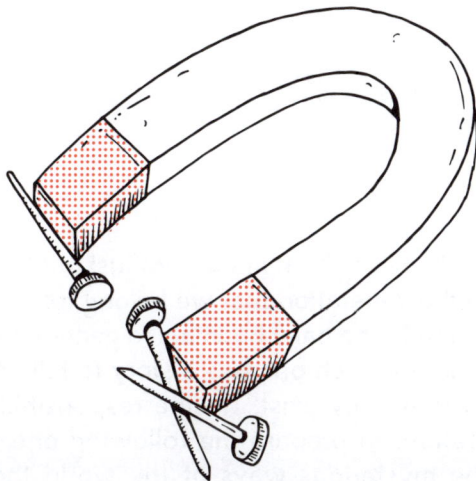

When we focus our thoughts on positive things, we get positive results. This law is based on the fact that people and everything that surrounds us is made from pure energy. This energy will attract the same kind of force we want to get back; it's our choice to pick between the positive vibes or the negatives ones. This goes perfectly with business, relationships, friendships and family matters. In the end, we are the captains of our destinies. And before we push away ourselves from the negative energy, we have to say...

Thankiou!

. . . .

The year in which we are born marks, not just our birth dates, but also the generation that we belong to. From the lost generation to the baby boomers to generations X , Y and millennials, each one has a story to tell and a reason as to why they exist. It's the responsibility of each generation, to prepare the following one to understand the mysterious ways of the world they leave us. That's the human chain that never ends. And before a new generation emerge, we have to say...

Thankiou!

THANKIOU #215
RELIVING IDEAS

Some researchers say that the average person has 70,000 thoughts per day. So, a lot of ideas are bound to fill our heads. Some ideas just stay as thoughts, others develop into conversations or written words, few become a reality, but most are forgotten. On odd occasions, we find ourselves in an uncommon dimension, and just like a puzzle, all the pieces align and an idea resurfaces. We then get all excited and start browsing through our minds to put the idea plan in motion once again. And before more ideas come up, we have to say...

Thankiou!

BEING THE HANDYMAN

The Do-It-Yourself modus operandi is tiring but enormously fulfilling. We can spend hours reading instructions, finding the pieces, buying the necessary stuff, figuring out how to put it together, but it all comes down to the end product. After a long day of wearing the handyman costume, we can stare into our masterpiece, show a timid grin at it and enjoy the hard work we put into. We can complete one project, but the household is an ongoing show. And before the next job for Mr. Handyman arrives, we have to say...

Thankiou!

THANKIOUS
217-230

THANKIOU #217
EXCERCISING AFTER A LONG TIME

Keeping a healthy body is key in living a long and fulfilling life. It's not all about work, money, cars and traveling, there's has to be a balance between it all. Playing some sports, going to the gym or just jogging can be very fundamental in keeping our bodies well and active. Sometimes we get caught in daily routines and forget to sweat a little bit, but Mother Nature is not forgiving and when we start again and suffer the consequences. And before the next sweating session, we have to say...

Thankiou!

THANKIOU #218
SPORTS FANATICS

The extended family of any sports team. These evangelists of the brand, players and system are the ones that make the team go to the championship level. They travel long miles to see their squad face off a fierce opponent, buy the official gear and wears them to work, collects their stuff, memorizes the players stats and doesn't miss the televised games. Fans are the beating heart of any team, as they go the team goes. And before more people become true fans, we have to say...

Thankiou!

Mom's homemade food is not always available. There are busy days when cooking or sitting down in a fancy restaurant are out of the question. What's left? Eating something fast, affordable and not necessarily from the brand name chains. Under that definition, food trucks, street vendors and local bistros are the ideal options. We can stop, order something -yummy and cheap- devour it and continue our lives without skipping a beat. And before we are hungry again, we have to say...

Thankiou!

THANKIOU #220
PASSPORTS

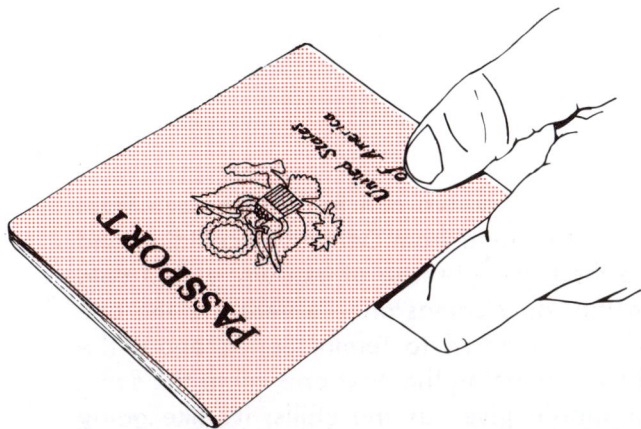

This little booklet is the key for crossing borders all around the world. Each country has its own passport for its citizens to use when they want to visit another country. It is required on the entrance of the nation, as a way to verify who and why is entering their borderlines. More so, passports are our own personal way of remembering all of our trips, because in each entrance it is stamped by the countries officials stamp. They are a diary of places. And before it expires, we have to say...

Thankiou!

. . . .

Through the window, we can feel the breeze from October and the wind from December colliding and creating a thrill. It's a breeze of its own, with a cold sensation that only comes once a year. It's the one time that we sit down to reminiscence about the year and start planning the next one, all at the same time. This month gives us the chills; it's like going back in time to feel what we felt as teenagers hearing 80's rock ballads and experiencing love for the first time. And before November ends, we have to say...

Thankiou!

THANKIOU #222
THE JOURNEY

It's a well-known fact that life is a journey, not a destination. Every time we plan something, the most encouraging moments happen before we even get a chance to accomplish the goal. The lead up to a kiss is a million times better than the kiss itself. Is in that 'in-between' where the learning's, experiences and failures reside. When we complete our objective, looking back at all the happenings will be the only thing we will take with us forever. And before we reach our final destination, we have to say...

Thankiou!

. . . .

It's a truly magnificent honor to see hundreds and hundreds of good vibes sent by friends and family members in a special occasion such as our birthdays. When we see them, it's almost unreal that people took time out of their busy lives and sat down to write, call or text something significant and beautiful. Good deeds are still part of our humanistic behavior, a clear sign that there is still hope in the world. And before our next birthday, we have to say…

Thankiou!

There is always, always something to be thankful for!

Unknown

THANKIOU #224
FREE STUFF EFFECT

Most man-made objects in the world have a price tag. Some are cheap while other are expensive, it all depends in the quality and the demand for it. However, in order to get us hooked on a particular brand, service or product, they give away free stuff to people. This practice makes us feel so special, we are willing to stand in long lines just to get the free item. Even though it's a great feeling, we cannot forget that nothing in this world is free. And before we've proudly used a promotional item, we have to say...

Thankiou!

· · · · · · · · ·

POINTS OF VIEW

Humans might share the same mold and overlap in a lot of fundamental things, but each one is their own unique planet. As a result, we have different passions, hobbies, interests, likes and dislikes. Diverse points of views make-up for an infinite amount of colors and options. It doesn't mean that some are better or worse than others, it means that no matter the differences we should always find ways to respect them all and learn to coexist in harmony. And before we share our way of seeing the world, we have to say...

Thankiou!

Local food represents the very core of any country. It has all the elements needed to understand the people's costumes and traditions. Tasting the food is like enjoying live history. These are generations and generations of recipes that have survived the test of time just to give us a matchless and distinctive flavor in every bite. When we enjoy our national food we are inviting our ancestors to the table. And before we brag about how good it is, we have to say...

Thankiou!

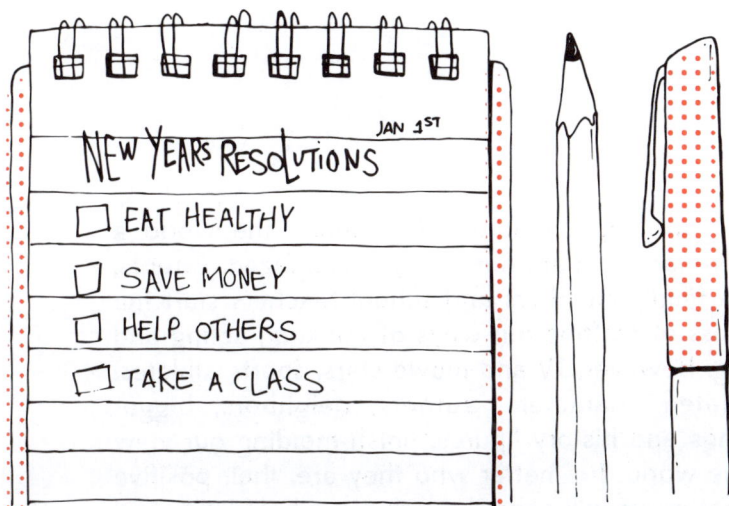

One of the most amazing things about starting a new year is making resolutions. Why? They are a breath of hope and a positive excuse to start over. It does not matter if our resolution is to learn a foreign language, start a new career, find love or start a low-fat diet; resolutions are crafted dreams and ideas with short-term deadlines that will spiritually and mentally make us better human beings. And if by this time of the year everything is falling into place, we have to say...

Thankiou!

CHILDHOOD HEROES

There are unsung heroes that make the world a better place and are not always recognized. Parents, close family members and school teachers start the process of crafting our ways of thinking, acting and doing. However, TV and movie stars, sports athletes, animated characters, authors, neighbors, bigger siblings and history figures, finish molding our view of the world. No matter who they are, their positive impact on us will echo through our whole lives. And before we hang a poster in our rooms, we have to say...

Thankiou!

THANKIOU #229
WINDOW SHOPPING

There are unsung heroes that make the world a better place and are not always recognized. Parents, close family members and school teachers start the process of crafting our ways of thinking, acting and doing. However, TV and movie stars, sports athletes, animated characters, authors, neighbors, bigger siblings and history figures, finish molding our view of the world. No matter who they are, their positive impact on us will echo through our whole lives. And before we hang a poster in our rooms, we have to say...

Thankiou!

. . . .

Not every day we have time to go to the market, pick fresh vegetables and meats, mix and match with herbs and spices and cook them to create an almost chef-like meal. Sometimes we only have thirty minutes to create something out of nothing, make it delicious, eat it and wash the dishes before everything is said and done. Although it is not ideal to do often, this fast-paced meals can save the day. And before we start the digestion, we have to say...

Thankiou!

THANKIOUS
231-244

THANKIOU #231
FOR BEING THANKFUL

There are a million reasons to be thankful, but not all them are recognized or accounted for. Every day is a gift, every smile a miracle and each of our friends and family members an excuse to be alive and well. Being thankful is more than a word or a sentiment, it is a state of mind. If we start acknowledging the miracles that we are blessed with, all the good will boomerang back at us. And before we eat some turkey, we have to say...

Thankiou!

THANKIOU #232
WHERE THE POSSIBLE AND THE IMPOSSIBLE MEET

For generations we have been taught that nothing is impossible, even the word itself says 'I'm possible'. That fine line between both words is surrounded by trial and errors, thinking outside the box, lots of imagination and much perseverance. We have learned that way past the impossible, there is a completely new storyline full of possibilities. Their meeting point is the exact place where life meets the unknown. And before they meet again, we have to say...

Thankiou!

. . . .

We built stuff with the hope of creating something that provides society with an alternative to be better. An entrepreneur once said that every problem is an opportunity to create a service or product that can change the world. But how we go from something good to something great? The answer is simple: friends to help us make it happen. And before we reach greatness, we have to say...

Thankiou!

THANKIOU #234
WHEN ANTIBIOTICS TAKE EFFECT

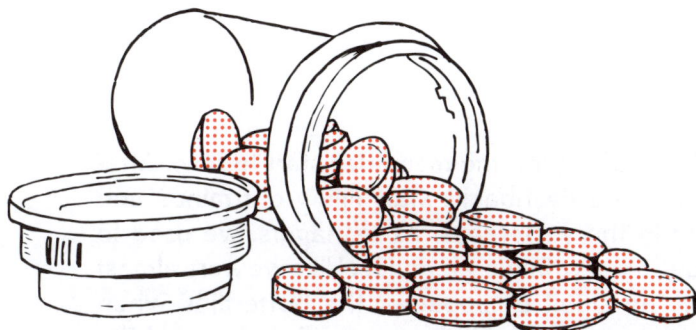

When we get sick, the viruses inside of us are either bacterial or viral, either way the best way to attack those viruses is with medicine. Days can pass and we can feel the same horrible way as if we didn't do something about it. When we finally decide to go to the doctor and he gives us a prescription of an antibiotic, our world of sickness turns around for good. It's a slow process, but we can feel how the headaches disappear, the runny nose isn't runny anymore and the throat comes to its senses. After three days, the world is beautiful again. And before the next time we go to the doctor, we have to say...

Thankiou!

· · · · · · · · ·

THANKIOU #235
OLD MOVIE THEATERS

From the parking lot, the memories start to flow. After we arrive, the flashbacks start filling our minds and basking in the yesterdays. As teenagers, we used to hang out, meet with friends and feel like we were almost adults. The smell of popcorn, the butterflies when seeing the girl we liked, the cool milkshakes and the ice cream round up an era that will never come back. Nevertheless, that old theater will always be where love started. And before the movie starts, we have to say...

Thankiou!

THANKIOU #236
WHERE EVERYONE KNOWS YOUR NAME

Small towns have the unique element of familiarity, anywhere we look there's someone who we know. More amazingly, in every coffee shop, restaurant, local pub or supermarket someone recognizes us. They know our name because of some past experience we shared at school, college, little league sports teams or lived nearby. It's a great feeling to be a known person in town. And before someone else calls out our name, we have to say...

Thankiou!

. . . .

Reasons for restoring faith in humanity: when people say I love you, thank you, please or any kind word, when someone rescues a complete stranger, peace after wars and storms, sportsmanship, long lasting friendships, helping sick animals get back on their feet, people helping people, feeding the hungry, when miracles happen, loving families sharing food at the table, making wishes come true, beautiful nature sights, thank you notes from strangers, free hugs, when all people are treated equally and saying I'm sorry. And before good deeds become the only deeds, we have to say...

Thankiou!

. . . .

WRITE AND DRAW YOUR
THANKIOU _____

Some movies are watched one time and forgotten, others we remember for forever. What makes a movie legendary is not just the actors or the special effects, it's all about the ending. The ending must include a scene with a speech we would love to memorize and repeat or an unexpected grand finale that leaves us wanting more. The last chapter is the do-or-die moment for any great film. And before the ending credits, we have to say...

Thankiou!

THANKIOU #239
STREETS WITHOUT POTHOLES

Driving can be both a stressful and therapeutic activity. Normally, when we get in the car we turn up the radio, the air condition and roll away like we are the kings of the roads. However, some things, like potholed streets, can make the ride less pleasurable and very obnoxious. When the roads are holes-free, the sensation inside the car is as we were hovering through the clouds without red lights. And before a tire brakes down, we have to say...

Thankiou!

Once in every lifetime a worthy man changes the track of life as we know it, for good. It may be an invention, speech, action, revolution or discovery, but It's a certainty that our lives will never be the same. They are titans that walk the Earth with the sole mission of overwriting the history books. The day they die, a little part of everyone dies with them. And before we say goodbye, we have to say...

Thankiou!

. . . .

THANKIOU #241
CLOSING UNEXPECTED DEALS

In the sales world, some days will bring great profits while other will suck so bad our motivation trembles. Nevertheless, nothing can stop us from dealing with new clients, taking risks and enjoying every single moment of it all. There will be days when everyone will say 'no' and others when no one will answer the phone, but in the mist of it all, someone unexpectedly will believe in us and say that striking 'yes'. And before we cash in, we have to say...

Thankiou!

· · · · · · · · ·

THANKIOU #242
CHOCOLATE OVERDOSE

Chocolate is one of the life's most pleasurable elixirs. First discovered by Mexico's Aztecs, it is well known for its aroma, aphrodisiac tendencies and medicinal purposes. Chocolate is so delicious and addictive that once we start eating it, there is no way to actually stop from enjoying its everlasting sweet taste. They come in all sorts of forms: truffles, syrup, bars, powder and in a cup. Once in a while, an overdose is not only necessary but imperative. And before chocolate becomes our blood type, we have to say...

Thankiou!

THANKIOU #243
IMPROVISATION

Improvisation is the art of creating something out of the blue. Often in life, some particular situations require our ability to improvise words to persuade, to get out of trouble, tell a story, act or even to make someone feel better. Not everyone can manage to do it, but those who can have an incredible power that comes with great responsibility. If used for the wrong reasons, it can hurt people, but if used as a weapon for good, it can lead to tons of laughs, memories and good times. And before the next show begins, we have to say...

Thankiou!

. . . .

Life is all about establishing relationships. Meeting new people is one of the few things that makes the world an interconnected place. When we are out there smiling, shaking hands, kissing babies, inventing jokes and laughing at the stories being told, we're making life happen. Networking is more than talking, is all about discovering people that we can help or can help us at some point in life. It is a technique that has to be developed, practiced and implemented in order to do it efficiently. And before we hand another business card, we have to say...

Thankiou!

THANKIOUS
245-261

THANKIOU #245
LAUGHING IN SILENCE

It's a fact that those who laugh alone are just remembering the naughty moments they have been involved in. These moments of imaginary déjà vu's can come without warning. Some pop up while in the shower, before going to sleep, while driving, sipping coffee or smoking a cigar. They all have one thing in common: they make us laugh just because. And before the next experience is remembered, we have to say...

Thankiou!

. . . .

THANKIOU #246
MUSIC ON SHUFFLE MODE

There is so much music variety that sometimes it's hard to choose one singer, band or genre. That's when we let the god's of music take over and become the DJ's of our imagination. Every song becomes a mystery selection -from our own personal library- that has the odd effect of being exactly the one we didn't know we wanted. After every shuffle, the one thing left for us is to embrace the unknown and sing along. And before the next random song comes on, we have to say...

Thankiou!

THANKIOU #247
SPECTACULAR VIEWS

When nature bonds with everything around it, a picture perfect moment comes alive. Only a few privileged places in the world can be labeled with the spectacular view title. The palate of colors, a clear skyline, the blend of sunlight with the clouds and the touch of God are the ideal elements to create an everlasting memory. As we stare into this view, we can only do two things: enjoy the beautiful scenery and pray it never ends. And before nature smiles back, we have to say...

Thankiou!

THANKIOU #248
HOMEMADE FOOD

Mom's homemade food is not always available. There are busy days when cooking or sitting down in a fancy restaurant are out of the question. What's left? Eating something fast, affordable and not necessarily from the brand name chains. Under that definition, food trucks, street vendors and local bistros are the ideal options. We can stop, order something -yummy and cheap- devour it and continue our lives without skipping a beat. And before we are hungry again, we have to say...

Thankiou!

. . . .

The clock hits the midnight mark and our stomachs begin to feel the other kind of butterflies. Although it's abnormal to feel hungry this late, the only thing going in our minds is something fatty, meaty and mouthwatering. We crave cheeseburgers, hot dogs, sandwiches, pizza, chicken tenders, french fries, ice cream or something in that greasy department. It isn't until we quench our hunger that life gets its color back. And before we exchange Chinese food for a bowl of cornflakes, we have to say...

Thankiou!

THANKIOU #250
THE NEXT LIFE

When the moment to leave the physical life comes, it's nothing more than a transition to a spiritual one. It might seem like a very sad moment for family and friends, but it is truly a celebration of a well-lived life. That day, we start to remember all the good times, the joyful and sad experiences, goals achieved and how fiercely we loved. In the end, all that matters boils down to what we did, how we did it and how it made the world a different place. And before we meet God in the next life, we have to say…

Thankiou!

. . . .

Being on the verge of one of the most sought out days of the year is magical. The miracle of happiness is expressed in every child that waits for the fat white beard guy. On this day, families gather to enjoy food, music and celebrate the waiting time. In the meantime, we reflect about the great things in life and the miracle of Christmas that brought us together again. It is without a doubt a great season to dance without a reason for it. And before Santa eats the cookies and milk, we have to say...

Thankiou!

. . . .

THE ESSENCE OF ALL BEAUTIFUL ART, ALL GREAT ART IS GRATITUDE.

Friedrich Nietzsche

THE HAPPIEST HOLIDAY OF ALL

Christmas time is the jolliest, happy, refreshing, playful, harmonic, delicious, awesome day of the year. Like it or not, our whole lives circulate around this merry time: we plan our yearly vacations during it, buy tickets to visit family, save money for the gifts and start the celebration two months in advanced. Jesus Christ not just sacrificed himself for our own lives, he did more than that, he gave us a full day every year of eternal happiness. And before it's December 26, we have to say...

Thankiou!

THANKIOU #253
FINDING OUR PASSION

Finding our true passion is one of the hardest challenges a human being will face in his lifespan. There are different kind of passion-finders: the ones who find it quickly, the ones who take more time, the ones who never acknowledge it, the ones who run tests to see them and the ones who come back for more. The great thing about finding our passion is that once we do it, life is seen through a different scope, we can't stop talking about it and there is not enough time to live it. And before we enjoy a lifelong vacation, we have to say...

Thankiou!

. . . .

These rock formations are born out of the combination of water and evolution. Caves are the mysterious side of the Earth and are only for those who dare to go a little deeper. Mother Nature's womb is filled with bats, crickets, snakes, stalactites, stalagmites, petroglyphs, paintings and undiscovered paths. At the beginning of time, Homo sapiens lived in them and with each visit we celebrate their lives. And before Batman's cave location is revealed, we have to say...

Thankiou!

THANKIOU #255
TEA

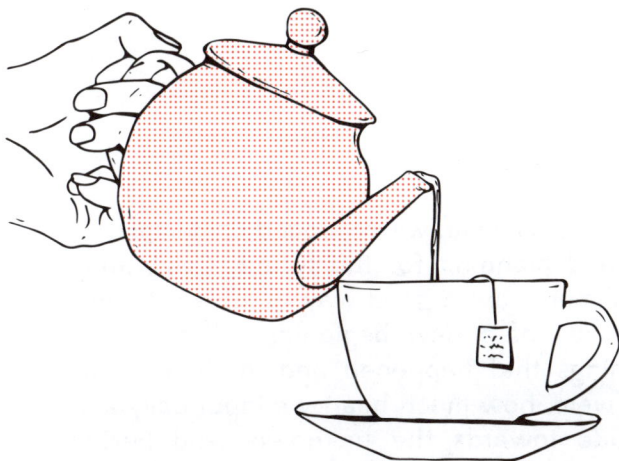

Coffee may be the alpha omega of hot beverages, but tea is something special. No one can say that they don't like it, because with so many blends, recipes, styles and flavors it is impossible one of them doesn't favor your palate. When we drink tea, our inner body is cleansed so deeply that everything relaxes and breathes new life. It is the secret formula to connect body, mind and soul, for a little while. And before we drink it all, we have to say…

Thankiou!

. . . .

At the end of each year, we sit around contemplating the past and planning for the future. Celebrating accomplishments are a good way to initiate a fresh start. The key of a new beginning relies heavily on the things that happened and mattered, how lucky we were, how much heart we input daily and our attitude towards the unknown. And before we say goodbye to yesterday, we have to say...

Thankiou!

THANKIOU #257
WALLS

One of the most ancient inventions in mankind's history. Walls have been protecting us since the eras of fire, fish and caves. Walls protect cities (The Great Wall of China), money (the bank safe), food (the walk-in freezers) and even the human body (the skin). They also create our own personal space in the world (houses, offices, bedrooms); they separate us from the world and transport us to our inner space. Could you imagine the world without walls? And for putting rocks together to form them, we have to say...

Thankiou!

. . . .

THANKIOU #258
THE CALM AFTER THE STORM

A storm can cause immeasurable damage to a town or country, but nothing lasts forever. After its heavy winds and unstoppable rains, the quiet time comes. At the moment, we get angry and frustrated with the situation that's upon us. Nonetheless, with a lot of patience and understanding of the circumstances, we comprehend that life gets the worst just before it gets a whole lot better. And before peace is achieved, we have to say...

Thankiou!

. . . .

HAPPINESS

is achieved
through
a grateful
heart.

Tasting a country's local beer is the same as drinking a part of their history. In this fermented juice, we can taste the water of their rivers and lakes, the spices, the generational recipes and the good times spent while enjoying it. Every moment is a good excuse to drink amongst friends and share experiences lived and those to be lived. And before we say cheers, we have to say...

Thankiou!

. . . .

THANKIOU #260
AUTOGRAPHS

Meeting someone famous is always a thrill. It could be a TV personality, writer, movie star, sports figure, singer or politician, but the best thing is to get an autograph from them. Pictures make great memories, but autographs say a little bit more. They often are accompanied of a personalized message or a small token of appreciation. And before we frame the autograph, we have to say...

Thankiou!

Before this generation, there was a group of pioneers who built our bloodline, land and nation. These ancient tribes left us a rich know-how in arts, astronomy, culture, gastronomy, and architecture. Our only remaining physical link to them is through the structures and drawings they created a long time ago. These discoveries have given us a better understanding of our past, in order to create a brighter future for all. And before we meet in the afterlife, we have to say...

Thankiou!

THANKIOUS
262-275

Fermented grape juice is an ideal companion to kick start any type of conversation. When this natural lubricant is in the mix, the topics can be very diverse and may include: past memories, business ideas, girlfriend troubles, cooking recipes, etc. The atmosphere can get seriously funny, very creative or even melancholic, but one thing will always stay true: wine tastes best when done among real friends. And before the bottle is empty, we have to say...

Thankiou!

THANKIOU #263
SLEEPING PILLS

Sleeping is one of the life's most enjoyable pleasures. Experts recommend that we sleep at least eight hours a day in order to obtain the necessary energy to function efficiently. However, not every day we get to sleep as much as we want or need, because of stress, excess caffeine, long work shifts or insomnia. When that happens, it's time to take a couple sleeping pills and disconnect ourselves from the world. And before the pills take effect, we have to say...

Thankiou!

Learning the fundamental techniques of a sport is very important in order to play it on a competitive base. When we get to master the basics, it's a matter of time before creativity hits us and the trick shots become a formality. Anything can become a possibility, from long distance shots to no-look passes, it all depends on how far we want to push the limits. And before we can duplicate the shot, we have to say...

Thankiou!

. . . .

THANKIOU #265
MONOPOLY MONEY

For us mortals, the game of Monopoly is the perfect opportunity to live the life of the rich and famous. With the free money we get, we buy land, trains, pay taxes, build houses, construct hotels and charge for them. After a while -and a with a little luck- we start exploring the bright side of capitalism as we collect money from other players and pile up enough of it to create an empire. And before the bank goes bankrupt, we have to say...

Thankiou!

. . . .

Waking up to the melody of someone telling us something we have been waiting for a long time, is endearing. Getting good news can change the mood and perspective of the day in a flash. There are a lot of good things that can happen: newspaper articles published, passing a test, not having to work, business milestone reached, a friend's success, promotions, problems solved, winning numbers of the lotto or a simple 'I love you'. In any of these cases, the word good could be insufficient to explain our smile. And before we start jumping in the bed, we have to say...

Thankiou!

THANKIOU #267
HUGGABLE PILLOWS

Pillows can be special companions. Sometimes they disguise as personal psychologists, best friends, secret keepers or huggable sidekicks. These stuffed blankets come in all sorts of shapes, colors, sizes and forms, but when we buy them, they become a unique piece that only we have. They can become a security and comfort partner in those cold, lonely and dark nights where all we need is to expel the melancholy and fear out of our systems. Huggable pillows are the millennials version of stuffed bears. And before the next stuffed bear comes alive, we have to say…

Thankiou!

There are millions of movies made and just a small percentage of them have a second part. Reasons to make a part two could be: a long story and divided it as in book volumes, a huge hit in the first one, making money or an idea that hit the director to create something anew. When the new movie is announced and the trailer released, we get anxious to see it. In most cases, sequels fail to fill our crazy expectations, but when they do, we can't stop talking about them and hoping that a third one will hit theaters soon. And before Rocky 88 premieres at the movie, we have to say…

Thankiou!

GRATITUDE
Towards
THE
MYSTICAL
• GENERATES •
MIRACLES

SURVIVING AN EARTHQUAKE

Earthquakes are natural disasters that are the result of a sudden release of energy in the Earth's crust that makes everything shake like crazy. Although it only lasts for a short period of time, those ten seconds can feel eternal. They are not very frequent but tend to be unpredictable and have an out-of-the-world force that strikes at different magnitudes. The only thing we can do is to duck for cover and pray for the best. And when the Earth stops shaking, we have to say...

Thankiou!

. . . .

THANKIOU #270
IDEAS INTO ACTION

There are moments in life when we need to shut up and put words into actions. We spend a lot of time talking and dreaming about going somewhere, starting a business, moving to a new city, going back to college or writing a book, but talking is the easy part. Living at the edge of the imagination leave us stuck in a cozy comfort zone. The hard part is, getting out there and actually doing it without fear of failure. And before we execute the plan, we have to say...

Thankiou!

THANKIOU #271
PAINTINGS WE LOVE TO STARE AT

Painting is an art that is only limited by the imagination. When an artist works its magic in a blank canvas, they transform nothing into beauty. Colors, techniques, brushes, paints, style and inspiration play a huge role in the makings of a work of art. When it's all said and done, the real triumph of the artist lies in the eyes of the admirer. If we can stare at it eternally, it can be called and labeled a masterpiece. And before we hang the painting in our living rooms, we have to say...

Thankiou!

THANKIOU #272
BUSINESS TRIPS

The world of business is a complicated one. As entrepreneurs, we have to look beyond our shores and explore the endless possibilities that exist far away. Business trips can be done for continued education purposes, visiting actual or potential clients, assisting a conference or expo, closing a deal or meeting suppliers. After work is done, it's all about having fun, exploring a new city and experiencing its culture. And before the tour bus picks us up at the hotel, we have to say...

Thankiou!

. . . .

THANKIOU #273
LIVING WHERE OTHERS VACATION

There's an island in the Caribbean that has the longest vacations in the world, the most number of holidays and, almost every day, a good reason to drink and have a good time. That island is Puerto Rico. Living in paradise is synonymous of beach campings, long lunches, networking events, road trip weekends, hangover Fridays and late night food truck stops. Everyone who lives in a place like this can easily say 'I live where you vacation'. And before the next Tuesday night spent socially drinking, we have to say...

Thankiou!

THANKIOU #274
BIOLUMINESCENT WATER

Astonishment is a common feeling when visiting one of the world's five bio bays at night. Bioluminescence is a light produced by a chemical reaction that occurs in a microorganism. These mysterious glowing things may even be responsible for some of the ghost stories told by sailors who witnessed the glowing waters but did not know the cause. Floating around these micro beings makes us witnesses of the magical power of ordinary things that are extraordinary in Mother Earth. And before the glowing stops, we have to say...

Thankiou!

THANKIOU #275
CATCHING UP WITH OLD FRIENDS

Real friends last forever. It doesn't matter if weeks, months or years have passed by, with them it's like time has moved in slow motion. While engaging in a meaningful conversation about love, life and business, it's imperative to have some kind of distilled spirit as a way to celebrate the moment. These convos seem continuous, like we picked up right where we left off. Distance will never be an obstacle in catching up with a friend, they are just one call, flight or visit away. And before the next bottle is opened, we have to say...

Thankiou!

THANKIOUS
276-289

Once in a while, friends get together to catch up on life and share their next moves. It's interesting to see and hear how a friend's thought went from just an idea to a concrete accomplishment in a short amount of time. Sharing plans are a useful way to get feedback, see the big picture and find a helping hand to guide us to success. Our hearts are filled with energy by just knowing that our advice paid off in a positive way. And before they hop in an airplane and get to Europe, we have to say...

Thankiou!

THANKIOU #277
THE ART OF CREATING THINGS

Every living thing on this planet is born with a God given talent. Discovering this skill is our life-long journey. It could be a single or a collection of things, for example: musical ear, painting intellect, math abilities, a knack for history, drive for business, the voice of an angel or the art of creating something out of nothing. There are a lot of aptitudes that we own, but there is just one that define us. It's our job to find it and exploit it to the max. And before we create the next big thing, we have to say...

Thankiou!

. . . .

We don't get the big idea by generating just one or a few, we need to create tons of them. But when that awesome idea comes up in a dream or pops in an unexpected moment, we get a rush of adrenaline. After getting the idea, we start building, shaping and optimizing it to produce a real tangible model. Once that's done, we are ready to share our vision with the world. And before more ideas pop up, we have to say...

Thankiou!

THANKIOU #279
BAD DAYS

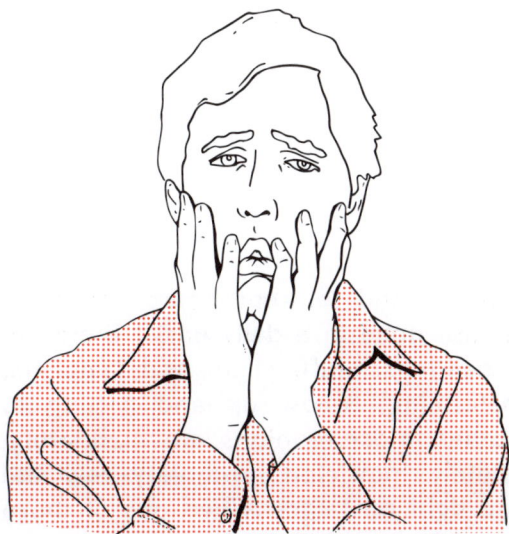

In life, there are good days and bad days, but it's in the bad days that we get to know ourselves. Through all the anger, bad luck, difficult situations, understandable faith and uncontrollable misbehaves, we can see a ray of hope. All these situations will allocate in a special place in our brains, giving us the understanding of all that could go wrong and how to fix it. It's always darkest before the dawn. And before the streak of good days start, we have to say...

Thankiou!

. . . .

For professionals and entrepreneurs meetings are a regular task done in a daily basis. There are all kinds of meetings: staff, client and suppliers, status, brainstorming, follow up and getting to know each other. Most reunions are mandatory, others completely inefficient and very few are successful and right on target. When one of those comes along and we hit the jackpot, it's just a matter of time for things to start happening. And before the next steps are done, we have to say...

Thankiou!

THANKIOU #281
WHEN FRIENDS GET AS OLD AS US

Time doesn't stop while we get a little bit older and experienced each day. Some of us reach adulthood and senior citizen age faster than others because we were born earlier. Getting older doesn't mean we are closer to death, it means we have had more time to enjoy life and share our experiences with those that will come after us. Birthdays are no longer about cake, they are about helping each other get to accomplish our dreams faster. And before the next friend's birthday party, we have to say...

Thankiou!

. . . .

THANKIOU #282
FOR BEING AT THE RIGHT TIME AND PLACE

Squeezed in the fast paced world we live in, there's a second where everything aligns. If we, by mere luck, find ourselves in that particular spot at the precise exact time we should, Miss Opportunity will knock at our door and slip us a wish. Nothing is as perfect like that moment when and we are part of something bigger than our surroundings. And before we find ourselves in the next right time, place and moment, we have to say...

Thankiou!

. . . .

If we replace nonsense with gratitude, life simplifies.

THANKIOU #283
THE RECIPE FOR HAPPINESS

We spend all our lives looking for our passion, our soul mate, a reason for existence and happiness. Just a few find one of them, but the truly great people formulate their own recipe for happiness. Deep in our soul resides the ingredients to a happy life, it's up to us to mix and match them right. After the preparation is done and we see the final product, we can enjoy all the big and little things that make our heart smile. And before adding more ingredients to the recipe, we have to say...

Thankiou!

. . . .

THANKIOU #284
BEING ON THE OTHER SIDE

There are two sides to every chronicle. Due to the circumstances of what we do, usually we tend to stay in one side wondering what the other side thinks and why they act the way they do. Rarely but surely, sides can change in the blink of an eye and we could find ourselves dreaming, negotiating, talking, hearing and doing stuff, at the other side. It's all fun and games when we are the ones in control and not the ones who are controlled by emotions. And before we switch sides again, we have to say...

Thankiou!

There are times in life where things can go from bad to worst in a blink of an eye. We can lose money in the market, have our house destroyed in a fire, fail an exam or get fired from a job, but we can't let ourselves down. It's up to us to persuade our inner selves that things are going to get better, that nothing is as important as health and life itself. Like the old saying, 'it's always darkest before the dawn'. And before the world unfolds as it should, we have to say...

Thankiou!

. . . .

THANKIOU #286
WORKING FROM HOME

When was the last time there was a Pajama Day at work? That's right, it has never happened. Working from home has great advantages, for example, we can wake up five minutes before we start the shift, don't have to dress up or get our hair done. The perks of working at home are that we have a homemade lunch break, nap in between tasks and we get to save gas and parking money. It's a win-win situation for everyone because it is an un-stressful atmosphere and, as a result, a very productive scenery. Studies concur that one day a week we should all work from home as a way to save some money, take care of the kids, help the environment and make work a more enjoyable experience. And before the next work day, we have to say...

Thankiou!

THANKIOU #287
VIBRANT WORKSHOPS

As professionals, we attend to a million of conferences, forums, expos, seminars and workshops, with the mindset that they will benefit positively our business and career. There's always something new learned, but just a few really change our whole perspective of how things are done and why they are made a certain way. If we scan around, we can feel the vibrant energy spreading all over the participants, and we can be sure that the presenter did more than his objective. And before we apply everything we learned to our day by day, we have to say...

Thankiou!

THANKIOU #288
DANCING ON STAGE

The thrill of dancing in front of a crowd resides heavily on the skill level of the dancers. If dancing is practiced routinely, we will feel like Hollywood stars. On the other hand, if both of our feet are not suited to move coordinately it could be a very embarrassing moment. There are a lot of ways we can end up on stage: picked by the presenters, drunk or challenged by a friend. No matter what happens up there, we will get an unforgettable experience out of it. And before the next dance off, we have to say...

Thankiou!

. . . .

Remembering is just a small part of reliving. When you can stare in the eyes of your past life in the here and now, it gives a meaning of fullness. All the good times comes back, the smiles, the smells and even that particular feeling. For some reason, we want to step back in time and enjoy the moment one last time, even if it's for old time's sake. And before we relieve the future, we have to say...

Thankiou!

THANKIOUS
290-303

An old Spanish proverb teaches us that hope is the last thing we lose. We have to fight until it hurts, swim against the current and see where there is no light, in order to get what we want out of life. It will not be an easy journey for a lot of us, but it will definitely be a lifetime experience to be told. When the world tells us to give up, let's try it one more time. And before we spread hope around us, we have to say...

Thankiou!

THANKIOU #291
ADMITTING MISTAKES

We are not always right. There are times that we might think one thing or do what we thought was the best possible scenario, but the reality is much more different. When things go the wrong way, the best we can do is to accept our mistakes and find solutions. It takes a lot of courage to take blame for something, but at the end it makes us stronger and prepare for the next battle. And before we amend our slip-up, we have to say...

Thankiou!

. . . .

THANKIOU #292
FOR NOT GETTING SICK

Flu and colds tend to be very, very contagious. When someone at the office or at home gets sick, we start washing our hands often, spraying antibacterial all over the place, drinking teas, taking vitamins, using hand sanitizer obsessively and evade them in order to avoid the illness. Not always the immune system works the way we would want it to, but when it does we feel like we dodge a bullet. And before we pop another preventive pill, we have to say...

Thankiou!

. . . .

THANKIOU #293
RIVALRIES

They are intense competitions between two different parts. Rivalries can be seen in almost every aspect of our daily life. We can see them in sports teams, political parties, businesses, siblings, friends and colleagues, among many others. These opposing challenges can last for days, years, even decades. In the end, no matter how heated or trivial a rivalry might be, the important thing is to show respect and honor the other side. And before we resume our battle, we have to say...

Thankiou!

. . . .

Since childhood, we are taught to follow every single rule on the book of life. There are rules for almost every aspect: school, home, self-imposed, talking, social behavior, religious and moral issues. In order to be a good citizen, we have to follow every single one of them. But sometimes, in order to live a little, we have got to get out of our comfort zone and break some of them. And before we actually break a rule, we have to say...

Thankiou!

THANKIOU #295
EMPTY INBOX

Read, answer, send, archive and repeat. Sometimes we got to do this over 100 times a day, every day. After we are done, we get that accomplished stress free feeling of getting stuff done. In order to keep our sanity, we have to come up with a system that fits our lifestyle and keep us away from becoming email slaves. Unsubscribing to unnecessary newsletters and databases is the first step to gaining back your sanity. And before we get a zillion more emails, we have to say...

Thankiou!

THANKIOU #296
JOKES WITH DOUBLE MEANING

There's a two side to every story and sometimes that other side has a filthy meaning. Life cannot be taken serious all the time, we have to sit back, relax and enjoy the show every time we can. Every now and then, joking with a hidden agenda is very witty and tricky. Some get them, others need to be explained, but at the end they are not meant to be offensive, just playful and fun. And before we send a mass text to all of our friends, we have to say...

Thankiou!

WRITE AND DRAW YOUR
THANKIOU _____

There have been found over 9,000 different types of fruits all around the world, but only one stands out of the pack. It's fruity, sweet, subtle and has a tropical taste that can only be harvested in exotic countries. This gift from Mother Earth is like no other. It's a known fact that those who don't like guava in any of its forms -fruit, juice, paste- haven't lived one day of their lives. And before the land produces the new crop, we have to say...

Thankiou!

THANKIOU #298
WHEN HEADACHES END

Having any kind of pain can transform a happy person into a moody one without being its own fault. Headaches can be caused by a lot of reasons, such as: being tired, not eating well, stress, sickness, being worried, needing caffeine or too much time in front of a computer. Either way, it's not fun at all to feel your head is about to explode in a million pieces. As a result, we put some ice on the forehead, take some pills, drink a coffee and wait. And before the medicine takes effect, we have to say...

Thankiou!

From time to time, we stumble with a startling circumstance that allows us to bring together people in order to create something. This 'AHA' moment is totally unexpected, but it usually is the missing puzzle piece to complete the big picture of life. Some people go from A to Z easily, but others need that final push to see the light at the end of the tunnel. That push is a combination of a friend's helping hand and a spark of destiny. And before the connection is made, we have to say...

Thankiou!

THANKIOU #300
SECRETS

Information is one of the most powerful things we know. Loading ourselves with important and valuable information can transform our lives and the ones around us. However, there is a VIP-kind of information called secrets. This information is more potent than any other, it's unique and only a handful of people knows it. Sharing top secret information is one of those things that create special bonds among people. And before we confide our most deep secret, we have to say...

Thankiou!

. . . .

THANKIOU #301
MINDSETS

The mind is the most influential element known to men. With it, anything and everything is possible or could become possible. Having the right set of ideas aligned the proper way can go a long way to develop and master a plan to success. If we wake up every day with a positive mindset, all the pieces of the puzzle of life will fall into place one by one. And before we adopt a life changing mindset, we have to say...

Thankiou!

. . . .

THANKIOU #302
MIRACLES

This phenomenon is driven by God's will and works in mysterious ways. We are all exposed to them often and constantly, but every once in a while there is a miracle that changes our whole existence. We hear stories about miracles that happen to other people and most of the time they are so incredible that they are almost unbelievable. Faith is the engine of this divine happening, so let's have it. And before we tell our most memorable miracle, we have to say...

Thankiou!

. . . .

THANKIOU #303
GETTING PUBLISHED

Writing is a grand way of eternizing words and thoughts forever. Having the words written down in a secret notebook isn't enough to show the world our mind, we need them to get published. It doesn't really matter in which format we got them printed: book, magazine, newspaper, blog, etc. It's a wonderful feeling to know that other people read our piece and that it could translate into a positive impact for them. And before we write our next masterpiece, we have to say…

Thankiou!

. . . .

THANKIOUS
304-317

THANKIOU #304
BEING ALONE WITH OUR THOUGHTS

There are times where is almost mandatory to disconnect from the real world and simply dive into our own emotions. When we enter nirvana everything starts making sense, decisions are made and we understand the way we have acted and the things we have done. It's not only about wishful thinking but about having a heart to heart with ourselves. We should always pick a few minutes every day to have some alone time and be with our thoughts. And before we space out, we have to say...

Thankiou!

. . . .

THANKIOU #305
BEING SURROUNDED BY NATURE

Entering the beauty of a tropical rainforest is one of the most spiritual experiences we can have. The sound of the birds, the cold waterfalls, the fresh air, the tall trees, the humidity, the diversity of living organisms, the rock formations and the palette of colors that Mother Nature wears. Those components combine to create a miniature version of paradise. Being deep inside the jungle is one of God's ways of hugging us. And before we get lost, we have to say...

Thankiou!

. . . .

From the farm to the plate. Being a chef is almost like being an artist, they both create masterpieces from scratch. The challenge is to pick the right ingredients, mixed them all together at exact quantities and cook them at precise temperatures to create something pleasant to the eye and palatable to the belly. And before we have to clean the big mess of the kitchen, we have to say...

Thankiou!

THANKIOU #307
MAGIC

Fact or fiction? This long seek answer has made the man play and use forces way beyond their understanding. Some say it is all an illusion created to amuse, but others have found it to be more than we can explain. There are all kinds of magic tricks and magicians, but all of them amaze us in their own unique way. Magic is an aphrodisiac for the eye and the extraordinary. And before we see a little bunny disappear in front of our eyes, we have to say...

Thankiou!

. . . .

Written in the most unpredictable of places, we can find a set of words that could make our day better. This unexpected messages can be found in an array of places like crosswords, billboards, banners hanging on bridges, inside crystal bottles, graffiti walls or mirrors written with lipstick. The idea of this message is not only to brighten our day but also to help us reflect on life and beyond. And before we decode an encrypted message, we have to say...

Thankiou!

THANKIOU #309
MUNCHIES

They fill the starvation gaps between breakfast, lunch and dinner. Munchies are hunger-quenchers in the form of sandwiches, candy, chips, beverages, popcorn, dips and hors d'oeuvre, among many others. They keep us energized and focused on the work or study we need to do to accomplish our daily goals. No eating moment is as sugary, greasy and tasty as the munchies time. And before it's munchies time again, we have to say...

Thankiou!

. . . .

It's a weird scenario when we hear recordings of ourselves talking and we don't tend to enjoy it at first. We press replay a couple of times trying to find the charm of it all. Sometimes it takes a while before we accept that what we are hearing is our real voice. After denial comes acceptance. Later, we start joking around, making fun of our accent, learning from the annoying habits and start getting pleasure from the melodic sounds that our voice emits. And before we start signing in karaoke, we have to say...

Thankiou!

HOW MANY
TIMES
CAN WE SAY
THANKIOU
IN
1 DAY?

We are surrounded by a million things to do, see and hear. It's easy to get distracted in this fast paced world we are living today. The true of the matter is that we need to focus on the things that will make our life happier, special and productive. We can procrastinate and waste a little time once in a while doing things that don't really matter, but at the end we need to sit down and get things done. And before we stress out about not doing what we are supposed to do, we have to say...

Thankiou!

THANKIOU #312
EXCUSES

A great way to not accept the truth is to give a justification. Excuses are born when we are too stubborn to accept reality. Although they might not be the best answer, they can help us stay out of trouble, make people happy instead of mad and sneak away from a difficult moment, among others. Excuses are for those who give them, but they help make life easier for all. And before we confabulate an epic excuse, we have to say...

Thankiou!

. . . .

We live surrounded by natural and man-made wonders, but some are easier to spot and admire than others. Every country has at least one particular wonder that leaves us amazed and eager to visit. It could be an ancient structure, a tall building, refined architecture, an invigorating tree or a technological marvel. Needless to say, each one is breathtaking and make us feel proud to be part of its countries history. And before the tour ends, we have to say...

Thankiou!

THANKIOU #314
CITY SKYLINES

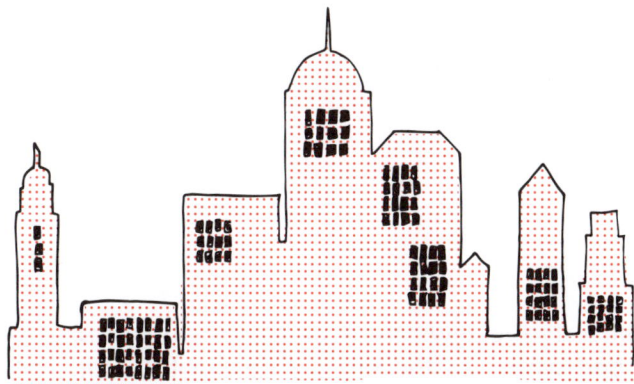

Metropolis tend to look less intimidating when we perceive them from the top. Skyscrapers look petite, cars go slow and people make us feel like giants. When we are on top of any tall building we can watch the mixture of the society from another perspective, for instance: social classes are well defined by altitude, light intensity and height of the structures, while public transportation seems non-stop and architecture plays a huge role in creating functional spaces for people to live efficiently. From the top, we can see parks, sports courts, the train system, vivid colors, the stars in space, airplanes are almost hand fetched, billboards from 100 miles away, houses of friends or relatives and places we didn't even knew existed. And before the cigar goes out, we have to say...

Thankiou!

People generated reviews are experiences evidenced in black and white. In the era before the Internet, everything was a word of mouth and we had to believe what the friend of the friend said to pick a place to eat or stay. Today, the digital revolution has created an invaluable tool of reviews were people write their experiences -either good or bad- so we can have an honest opinion and not a marketing generated one. This has elevated the bar for many establishments. And before we stay at a five star rated hotel, we have to say...

Thankiou!

. . . .

THANKIOU #316
THE UNKNOWN

In life, there is no direct road to happiness, success and good fortune. Nobody knows what's in store for each one of us and there is no way to know what will become of us tomorrow or in ten years from now. All we know is that in the mystery of life, there are a lot of opportunities to create meaningful and beautiful things that can last a lifetime. And before the unknown becomes the known, we have to say...

Thankiou!

. . . .

When we sell an idea, product, service or dream, very often we will hear the word 'no'. It's almost a norm that most business executives are trained to say this word, the most depressing of the dictionary before someone convinces them otherwise. There is no recollection as to why this happens, but a lot of studies have been focused into changing this mindset. It's all about making the words come together while we hold our heart in our hands. And before we hear the yes, we have to say...

Thankiou!

THANKIOUS
318-331

THANKIOU #318
COMPLETING RESOLUTIONS

Over the course of the year, we tend to make plans and resolutions that we don't really follow. However, certain people, songs, movies and books make us refocus and boost our energy to complete them. This second step to success can be used to continue writing the book we started, fall in love again with a collection we own or renew the membership of the tango dance class. It doesn't matter the road we choose as long as we reach out for the grand finale. And before we re-ignite some old passions, we have to say...

Thankiou!

. . . .

THANKIOU #319
GOD'S GIFTS TO HUMANKIND

Over 2,000 years ago, the greatest faith act on Earth was done by a single man. Although, God's son Jesus, was no ordinary human being, he lived like one of us. He was truly a dreamer that dreamed of a better tomorrow for everyone. He came to this planet with the sole mission of giving his brothers a better lifestyle and in his path he took the road less traveled and gave up his life for us. Needless to say, he changed the course of history forever. And before he resurrects again, we have to say...

Thankiou!

· · · · · · · · ·

There is no doubt that food is one of the life's greatest pleasures. The only drawback of abusing this pleasure is the bad effects it has on our health. In order to still have them and not getting fat we have invented mini sized versions of our most beloved foods like hamburgers, burritos, pizza, cupcakes and donuts, among others. These small and delicious bits makes us feel like giants and help us stay fit. And before we order mini size combo, we have to say...

Thankiou!

. . . .

THANKIOU #321
CROSSROADS

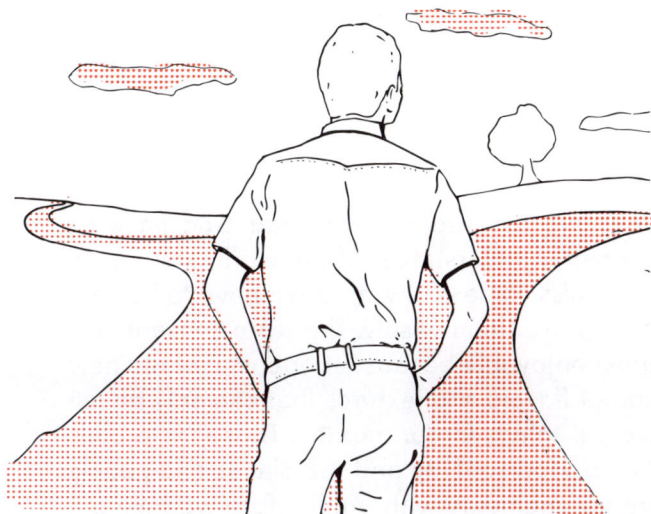

Once upon a time, someone came up with the phrase 'life is like a box of chocolates, you never know what you are going to get'. It is as truth as it sounds, there's no sure way to know where we are going to be tomorrow or in five years, but the important things stay forever inside us. That's why, when two real friends find each other in life's crossroads, it's a truly inspiring moment to share. And before we continue our paths, we have to say...

Thankiou!

. . . .

The senses are the superpowers that God gave us to have a better understating of the world around us. Some of us miss some of them, so we have to be very thankful and use them wisely. The taste sense is one of the most enjoyable because it opens a whole new dimension of flavors and textures that can only be felt when we put things in our mouths. Those taste buds can define our personality and the places and people we share our moments with. And before we take out our tongue to enjoy some ice cream, we have to say...

Thankiou!

. . . .

**Every
second,
every
step,
&
every
moment
are
more than
enough
reasons to be
thankful.**

THANKIOU #325
UNFINISHED BUSINESS

In life, there are moments that are left up in the air. They were started but never concluded. There are millions of things that can be left incomplete like a romance, project, dream or goal. Nonetheless, when something is left unfinished, life sometimes gives us one more chance to return, un-pause and seal the deal once and for all. If we allow it to stay incomplete, we run the likelihood of forever living with the dreadful 'what if?' And before we pick up the phone to resolve the past, we have to say...

Thankiou!

. . . .

THANKIOU #326
REFUSING TO GROW UP

Being young and full of energy is much more than age, it is a state of mind. Although, these are the years in which we develop into the person life has set us to become, it's kind of short lived. That's why unconsciously, we refuse to accept reality by wearing teenager clothes, dye our hair, use makeup to disguise age, re-watch programs that remind us of a better time, among others. While we remain in denial, Father Time reminds us that life goes on. And before we start growing gray hair, we have to say...

Thankiou!

THANKIOU #327
THE FEELING OF REALIZATION

There are a few key moments in life where we feel fully satisfied with what we have accomplished. Finishing school, getting a job, retiring, publishing a book, traveling to a dream destination, putting a smile on a sad face - are just a few. In that instant, we look straight up, put the biggest smile on our face and let the stress monkey leave us for good. It's a good day to be alive. And before we tell our grandkids, we have to say...

Thankiou!

. . . .

THANKIOU #328
EATING LIKE THERE IS NO TOMORROW

The animal instinct that humans have is still alive in the way we eat when we are hungry. There is no courtesy, manners or protocol just a killer instinct to devour any food put in front of us. We know it's time to eat when we feel without energy, sick or are turning pale. After we finish the meal that ended our misery, a satisfying and conquering smile is drawn in our faces until the next feeding. And before we roar in celebration, we have to say…

Thankiou!

. . . .

THANKIOU #329
MEETING OUR IDOL

For as long as we remember, we have dreamed about being in their shoes. We have seen their movies, read their books, watched every single game and sang their songs in karaoke, but none of those experiences compares to the moment when we finally meet them in person. The sensation of exchanging words and hugging them is out of this world. And before we ask for an autograph, we have to say…

Thankiou!

. . . .

THANKIOU #330
PARENTAL FIGURES

There is Mother's and Father's day, but there isn't a special day for celebrating that person who acted like a parent but wasn't the real one. They took on the responsibility of raising a child that wasn't theirs like it was their own. Anyone could become this parental figure, a stepparent, grandparent, uncle, sibling or even a neighbor. In the end, it doesn't really matter who is who, the important thing is the love that surrounds and creates a happy household. And before we produce a new holiday, we have to say...

Thankiou!

THE BEGINNING OF TIME

History shows that God created us in the sixth day and one day later he finished its masterpiece. The creation of humanity -as we know it- should have been glorious and more than magical. Thanks to that and with a little help of Adam and Eve, we are here today basking in our own existence. Anyhow, the question remains, why are we here? The answer to this complex question might be the key to life. And before we start searching for the answers, we have to say...

Thankiou!

. . . .

THANKIOUS
332-345

The sun might not have come out yet, but the phone is ringing, the texts are coming in and the emails are piling up. The only explanation for this kind of behavior is that something good has emerged and it's in the world. That smile that comes out naturally when you read the first congratulations, it's just the necessary boost to make an ordinary day an extraordinary one. And before we get out of bed, we have to say...

Thankiou!

THANKIOU #333
WHEN SOMETHING FITS

God has a time and place for everyone and everything. It's no coincidence that certain things tend to blend the right way without an explanation. Sometimes it takes time to understand that in order to make it fit, we have to align with the world around us. It's just a matter of time when we realize that some people were meant to be together, not just because it makes sense but because they fit the right way. And before we try it on, we have to say...

Thankiou!

. . . .

THANKIOU #334
WANTING MORE

When reaching for the stars isn't good enough, we have to fetch even further to truly find ourselves. The passion and ambition of wanting more out of life is just a primitive reflect of the Homo sapiens race. In that purpose, emotions flourishes and expresses itself in the purest of forms. When passion blossoms, we evolve as persons and species; that's why, we always want more. And before we get some, we have to say...

Thankiou!

THANKIOU #335
HEART TO HEART CONVERSATIONS

Once in a while one of our beasties needs to let it out and talk it out. Chatting from the heart does not always involve lovers or family members, it can be a special moment between friends. We know when it's happening, we can feel the vibe, the tone and the openness of the moment. Having these talks brings out our true selves and automatically expels the best in us. When we talk from the heart, our souls start listening and the mind absorbs the positive energy needed to send the body into neutral. And before the tête-à-tête ends, we have to say...

Thankiou!

PROCRASTINATION

There are days when we don't feel like doing the things we are supposed to do and instead we do all the things we shouldn't be doing. Although it might seem like a waste of time, we are spending it doing other stuff we enjoy to do in our spare time. The dire thing about procrastinating is not getting done the things we need to do, but if you do them, then it's all good. And before we start doing nothing, we have to say...

Thankiou!

. . . .

THANKIOU #337
JUST BECAUSE

Sometimes there are just no reasons at all to be or not to be. Just because life is beautiful -with all its imperfections- is enough reason to be grateful. To be thankful is to be in peace with our surrounding and ourselves. Our time here on Earth is the biggest gift of all and everything we take with us -good or bad- into eternity is more than enough to be pleased and in peace. And before we even think about it, we have to say...

Thankiou!

. . . .

THANKIOU #338
FIGHTING WITH A CONSCIENCE

Life is a long bumpy road where thing's may not turn out as planned. There are a lot of injustices and wrongs that surround our everyday, but it's up to us to let our voices be heard and fight the cause. It's not about war or violence, it's about morals and principles. When something is not done right, we need to stand up and find the road to the truth. And before we deliver an everlasting message, we have to say...

Thankiou!

. . . .

Be **thankful** for what you have;
you'll end up having more.

If you concentrate on what you don't have, you will never have enough.

Oprah Winfrey

When something starts new, there is no way to know how successful it will be. The one thing standing between an idea and a real business, it's to get the first customer to believe in what we believe and buy it. This step is the first step to the rest of our lives. And before we frame the first dollar, we have to say...

Thankiou!

THANKIOU #340
KARMA

What we do in the present has a direct reflection on the future. That means that every decision, action or deed we do will come back to us in a boomerang fashion. In order to get good things back, we have to do good things, but if we do things the wrong way they will bounce back and bite us. Karma defines our destiny and only we can steer it the right way. And before we dodge bad karma, we have to say...

Thankiou!

THANKIOU #341
PROTOTYPING

Climate change is an uncontrollable force of nature where we have no choice but to adapt to it. When Mother Nature speaks we have to listen thoroughly and make the best out of the worst. As the spring season leaves and summer arrives, it tags along the heat and humidity that makes us feel like we are going to melt. We can trick the weather with air conditioning and fans but at the end, all we can do is survive. And before the summer is over, we have to say...

Thankiou!

· · · · · · · · ·

THANKIOU #342
COMPETITION

"What doesn't kill us, makes us stronger". Having rivalry is not usually a negative thing, it is a great excuse to be constantly innovating and trend setting. When we own a business or train for an athletic contest, falling into the comfort zone is not an option. We have to always be in the lookout for the opposition and the leaders in order to outperform them in a positive and creative way. And before we buy out the competitors, we have to say…

Thankiou!

. . . .

We have to get up, get out and start shaking our bodies in order to have a healthier and longer life. The first step is always the hardest but once we take it, everything else falls into place. The combination of excitement, new shoes and adrenaline will make up for the out-of-shape lungs and helps us through the workout. Nonetheless, the next day pain will be at its highest peak, but at the end, our body and mind will be grateful. And before we call the paramedics, we have to say...

Thankiou!

· · · · · · · · ·

THANKIOU #344
HOTEL ROOMS

Hotels are the closest thing to our homes when we are away from them. They have everything we need without the hassle of cleaning or making the bed. Nowadays, rooms are packed with TV's, iPod stereos, pod coffee makers, mini bar, feathers filled pillows, Jacuzzi, Wi-Fi and room service. They may not have our beds smell, but their luxurious and detail oriented infrastructure makes up for it. And before we go back to the convention hall, we have to say...

Thankiou!

. . . .

In some cultures, more than one name is acceptable and middle names are often used between the first name and the surname. Although they are often forgotten in conversation, they give us a more authentic identity of who we are. A lot of people can have the same first and last name but having the same middle name is not usual. These names can be hereditary, in tribute to an ancestor, a joke between parents or a way to make our names seem more sophisticated. And before we name our children, we have to say...

Thankiou!

THANKIOUS
346-365

THANKIOU #346
PREPARING FOR SOMETHING BIGGER THAN LIFE

We constantly question our place on Earth and our purpose in life. Just to find out that we have been preparing for that purpose since the day we were born. Some paths are rockier than others, but at the end the world tends to unfold as it should be. It doesn't matter if we turn out to be a scientist, artist, entrepreneur or family man, we are essential to everyone's existence in this world. And before our time comes, we have to say...

Thankiou!

. . . .

THANKIOU #347
SURVIVING THE HEAT

Climate change is an uncontrollable force of nature where we have no choice but to adapt to it. When Mother Nature speaks we have to listen thoroughly and make the best out of the worst. As the spring season leaves and summer arrives, it tags along the heat and humidity that makes us feel like we are going to melt. We can trick the weather with air conditioning and fans but at the end, all we can do is survive. And before the summer is over, we have to say...

Thankiou!

. . . .

There's no doubt that technology has brought us closer, making the world a smaller place. Having the ability to see and talk to someone that's a thousand miles away is endearing. It sometimes feels as if they are not far, but close to us. We can see, hear and almost feel that special someone on the other side of the monitor, phone or tablet and feel comfortable, safe and happy. And before we lose the connection, we have to say...

Thankiou!

THANKIOU #349
BREAD OUT OF THE OVEN

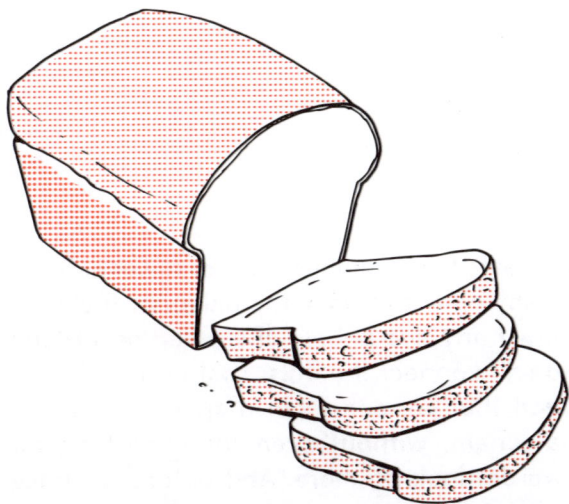

Bread is one of the humanity's oldest foods, it's most recognizable and popular. This delicacy is made out of a combination of flour, water and love. After careful preparation, it can transform into a zillion forms and combine with a lot of ingredients to create a luscious complement to any meal, conversation or wine pairing. Its flavor can be at its best when we eat it straight out of the oven when it's still soft, warm and doughy. And before we actually break some bread, we have to say...

Thankiou!

· · · · · · · ·

This theory states that everyone is six or fewer degrees away from any other person in the universe. If we are set to connect any two people, the chain of a friend of a friend will connect the dots. Lost in that theory, is the notion that we can meet a special someone within that chain, without even trying to look for it. Once we do, look no more. And before we trace on how we got to meet everyone, we have to say...

Thankiou!

THANKIOU #351
WHEN A FRIEND BECOMES SOMETHING ELSE

For years we can have all the answers in front of us, but for some mysterious reason we cannot see them. However when the right time comes, the world gives us all the necessary signals to overcome this blindness and make a move. This often happens with friends that all along we know we love, but are too dumb to realized it or do something about it. Oh, but when we do it, life will never be the same. And before we fantasize how different the past could have been, we have to say...

Thankiou!

. . . .

As professionals, we have to follow society's rules and perform business etiquette with finesse. Every day comes and goes with problems to be solved, challenges to surpass and complicated tests that life puts in our path. Sometimes we get so overwhelmed that we just need to let it out and pretend we are not from the normal world. It is in this imaginary flight to nowhere that everything makes sense when we start talking nonsense. As a result, laughter and craziness will be created and spread around. And before we convert nonsense into something with sense, we have to say...

Thankiou!

. . . .

THANKIOU #353
TAKING CONTROL OF OUR DESTINY

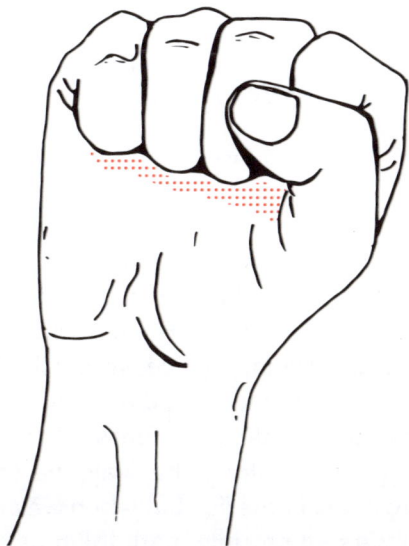

There are some defining moments in life where we have to stop pretending and just start focusing on the important things. Among the things we have to do there are: picking a lifestyle, searching for passions, drawing a plan, describing the best scenario and preparing mentally and spiritually for tomorrow. Nobody said life was going to be an easy ride, but we have to start somewhere. And before we press the cruise control button, we have to say...

Thankiou!

. . . .

As we look towards the future, we ask ourselves, what do we want to accomplish in life? The first step is to create a numbered list of all the things. For example: travel to all the wonders of the world, skydive, attend the Olympics, climb Mt. Everest, write a book, date a foreigner, catch a wave in Hawaii, create a business or be front page news, among others. Along the way, we can add or subtract more items to the list, but when we accomplish any of them we can proudly mark them as done. And before we complete the whole list, we have to say...

Thankiou!

. . . .

THANKIOU #355
FINISHING A BOOK

We get to read a book because the cover looks interesting, a friend recommended it, it is a bestseller or we enjoy very much the main topic. Either way, we have no clue in what to really expect from the story, but we hope it is one that captures our imagination. After reading the first few pages, we know if we are falling in love with it or just leaving it to die at our coffee table. But when a character's story becomes our own, there is no looking back. And before we join a book club, we have to say...

Thankiou!

. . . .

Human beings have always been keen with the unknown. There are all kinds of surprises: the ones that make us anxious, the ones that scare us, the ones the makes us smile and the ones we have no clue in what to expect. Good or bad, they make our heart beat in a fast and uncontrollable way. As a way to preserve the essence of the shock, hints and clues are not allowed but encouraged. And before the surprise is revealed, we have to say...

Thankiou!

THE WORLD CAN
BE CHANGED
ONE
THANKFUL
ACTION AT A
TIME.

When we are playing a game we have to be prepared for a 50-50 chance of succeeding or failing. In order for the game result to have a logical outcome, one side has to come out victorious and the other has to handle the difficult task of losing. Not everyone can be on one side of the equation. If we find ourselves on the winning corner -just after the final buzzer- we have no other option than to smile and be proud that all the hard work paid off. And before the next game starts, we have to say...

Thankiou!

. . . .

THANKIOU #358
SECOND CHANCES

Rarely in life we get a second opportunity at something we missed, lost or ignored. When we miss the boat, it doesn't stop just for us. However when life rewards us with a second chance, we cannot blink at the opportunity and should jump at it right away. There is no worst thing than to live a life full of 'what ifs'. And before no more chances are given, we have to say...

Thankiou!

There is no doubt that sugar is the magic powder of the gods. It is an addictive force often found in desserts. The only bad thing about sugary desserts is that they will make us gain a few unwanted pounds. As a solution, a great invention was made: a mini version of the whole desserts. They have the same blast of flavor but a fraction of the calories. And before we eat too many, we have to say...

Thankiou!

THANKIOU #360
THE FIRST TREE

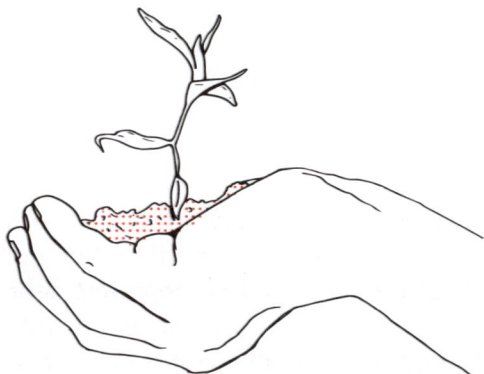

Age-old legends say that we shouldn't leave this life without: planting a tree, writing a book and having a child. It's an amazing feeling to know that in a couple of weeks -with lots of water- new life will burst. Consequently, giving Mother Earth a new child to nurture, grow and create a more sustainable environment for all living forms in our Planet. That tree will become an extension of our own life's and a never ending memory that will stand tall even after we are gone. And before it sprouts, we have to say...

Thankiou!

. . . .

There's an explanation for every little aspect of our lives. It is just a matter of putting the right combination of letters and symbols together. When we ask something, the only outcome expected is an answer. Although there is no wrong answer, we always have certain expectations. But when we do get the expected answer, a new world opens up. And before we run out of questions to ask, we have to say...

Thankiou!

THANKIOU #362
SHORTCUTS

There might not be shortcuts in life, but they sure are everywhere else. Shortcuts are convenient and alternative routes that tend to be shorter and more effective. We can greatly benefit from these shortcuts when we are driving to skip traffic jams. In order to make them work, we need to know the city as it was the palm of our own hands. Once we reach our destination in half the time it normally takes, we can feel proud. And before the shortcut is no longer a secret path, we have to say...

Thankiou!

. . . .

While eating, we use all of our senses to form general judgments, but it is the taste that is the most influential in deciding how delicious the food is. Traditionally, it has been thought that our sense of taste is comprised of four basic tastes -sweet, sour, salty and bitter. However, it is now known that there is a fifth taste called umami. Most people might not recognize this fifth flavor but when we encounter it, we'll be in the presence of a mouthwatering experience. And before umami takes over, we have to say...

Thankiou!

THANKIOU #364
REMEMBERING NAMES

What is his/her name? Sometimes we can't remember but, as social behavior teaches us, we engage in a very challenging small talk conversation. We find ourselves asking about professional endeavors, family and mutual friends, not just because we care but as a way of finding a hint of who they are and where do we know them from. The positive thing about this is that people recognize us, taking time and energy, to exchange words and smiles for the sanctity of past, present and future life experiences. Keep in mind that life is all about establishing relationships. And when that name pops in our head, we have to say...

Thankiou!

· · · · · · · · ·

Every day we are gifted is a new reason to express, in our own particular way, how thankful we are of all the small and exceptional things that happen and have a huge impact in our day to day. Being thankful for the good, bad, weird and ordinary stuff that occurs to us daily is more than an idea, it's a lifestyle. It may not last for eternity, but for as long as it lasts, we have to make the best of it. And before we say thank you over and over again, we have to say...

Thankiou!

. . . .

AND BEFORE
EVERYTHING IS
SAID & DONE
WE HAVE TO SAY...
THANKIOU!

ABOUT THE AUTHOR
PAUL E GONZÁLEZ

A Generation Y writer, published poet, day dreamer, hopeless romantic, avid blogger, fun facts reader, award-winning entrepreneur, endless hustler, event producer, non-practicing accountant, Guinness World Record holder, future professor, microwave chef, foodie at heart, whiskey enthusiast, coffee addict, world explorer, beach bum, skim board rookie, basketball cards collector, San Antonio Spurs fan, wannabe magician and retired skateboarder from the Caribbean island of Puerto Rico.